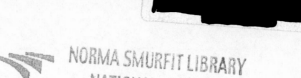

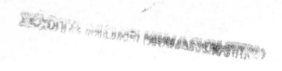

Ireland *and the* European Union

The First Thirty Years, 1973–2002

Edited by Jim Hourihane

THE LILLIPUT PRESS
DUBLIN

First published 2004 by
THE LILLIPUT PRESS LTD
62–63 Sitric Road, Arbour Hill,
Dublin 7, Ireland
www.lilliputpress.ie

A CIP record for this title is available
from The British Library.

1 3 5 7 9 10 8 6 4 2

ISBN 1 84351 035 9

Published with the support of
The Communicating Europe Initiative, Department of Foreign Affairs
and The Research Committee, St Patrick's College,Drumcondra.
The editor also wishes to acknowledge the
support of Urban Institute Ireland.

Set in Perpetua
Printed in Dublin by ßetaprint

Contents

FOREWORD BY COMMISSIONER DAVID BYRNE   vii

INTRODUCTION BY JIM HOURIHANE   xv

1. *The Dynamics of Membership*
    JIM HOURIHANE   1

2. *Changing Times, Changing Cultures*
    MICHAEL CRONIN   12

3. *Irish and European Law*
    CATHRYN COSTELLO   26

4. *People, Work and Social Change*
    DAVID BEGG   40

5. *Irish Politics and European Politics*
    BRIGID LAFFAN   54

6. *The Economics of EU Membership*
    GARRET FITZGERALD   67

7. *Europe, Democracy and Ireland*
    LARRY SIEDENTOP   81

8. *Ireland and Europe: Embracing Change*
    BERTIE AHERN   94

NOTES   107

ACKNOWLEDGMENTS   113

NOTES ON CONTRIBUTORS   115

Foreword

I am honoured to provide the foreword to this timely publication of Thomas Davis lectures on Ireland's first thirty years of membership of the European Union. The broad range and scope of the lectures raise issues that remain pertinent to the present and also provide us with a valuable insight into the challenges that await the Union and its new members as it prepares for its largest ever enlargement to twenty-five countries on 1 May 2004. On reading many of the contributions I was struck by the progress that Ireland has made since, and as a result of, its membership of the Union. It is easy to forget, indeed, that in the early 1970s economic and social conditions in Ireland were a far cry from those in today's modern society. Consumer, environmental and equality legislation, such as it was, was minimal. Ireland was a country resigned to emigration to solve its many economic and social problems. The process through which Ireland changed in the years following membership, and how it adapted to its obligations as a member of the European Community, can indeed be an inspiration to those states that are now preparing to assume the challenges of membership.

A Union Based on Treaties and Law
My background being a legal one, I was naturally attracted to the contribution of Cathryn Costello in 'Irish and European Law'.

The impressive list of environmental, social and equality issues outlined in her lecture as having an origin in EU law serves to highlight the hugely important role that the Union has played in introducing change and progress in Ireland. I was particularly struck by the estimate that 60 per cent of all Irish law has developed from EU legislation. Of course, it must be emphasized time and again that EU laws do not suddenly appear overnight to be implemented by national governments. Whether laws emerge from Treaties, Regulations or Directives, an extensive consultation process involving the governments of the member states and the EU institutions precedes them all. In many cases nowadays, legislative proposals are made by the Commission at the behest of the European Parliament or of member state governments or are designed to implement broad policy initiatives that have already been agreed, notably at European Council level. Creation of laws that require wide consultation is not an automatic process and many changes are introduced to original proposals to take account of the concerns of individual member states. Indeed, on occasions proposals may be abandoned in their entirety. The image therefore of a faceless bureaucracy in a far-away city imposing strange rules on nation-states could not be further from the truth.

The Irish 'Space'

Too often, when assessing the impact of EU membership on Ireland, attention concentrates exclusively on economic and social benefits. Of course it is accepted that the Irish social and economic landscape has been transformed by membership. The approach of geographer Jim Hourihane, to look at its impact on the Irish 'space', presents us with a thought-provoking view from another angle. I was impressed by the argument of Mr

Hourihane that indeed the Irish 'space' has also undergone change as a result of membership. He points out that our environment is the product of interaction between space, time, people and politics. Looked at from this point of view, it was inevitable that the introduction of a European dimension to politics and policy-making would result in changes to our environment. Thirty years after membership few could contest that there have been significant changes to our overall living environment and that many of these were generated from our membership of the Union. And few would argue that such changes have been other than for the better. The EU has been to the forefront in advocating and legislating for a better environment. It would be interesting to contemplate the Irish landscape today after many years of industrial development, had strong environmental standards not been in place to control and guide this development. But this is an ongoing challenge and requires vigilance at both national and EU levels.

Connecting with the Citizen

The European Union is founded on the basis of a number of treaties and a great deal of legislation. But laws and treaties do not of themselves create acceptance among the general population. It is necessary that the citizens of Europe feel that they are part of the European process before the legitimacy of the Union can be fully accepted. Communication and information on Europe and European issues is essential. This point is made forcefully by Professor Brigid Laffan in her lecture 'Irish Politics and European Politics'. The rejection of the first referendum on the Nice Treaty highlighted the need to inform the public of the issues involved. No electorate can ever be taken for granted and the Irish electorate, before the second referendum on Nice, made a conscious effort to familiarize itself with the provisions of the Treaty. Once they became more familiar with the issues they voted more enthusiastically and positively than they had in the first referendum. This shows that Europe can be made relevant to people's lives and that they are willing to engage with it if provided with the opportunity to do so.

This is indeed one of the most crucial issues facing the European Union as it moves towards adoption of a new Treaty that will require fundamental changes to how the Union works, its institutions, and its competencies. The lessons of the first referendum on the Nice Treaty still ring clear. They are that the citizenry must be engaged and the implications of the new Treaty must be explained to them in a sustained way over time. More than that, a widespread debate must take place to ensure that all views are heard and evaluated. And this debate must be led by politicians, including MEPs, trade unions, employers' bodies, NGOs and other civil society groups.

From Independence to Interdependence

Over thirty years, from being a somewhat isolated island on the periphery of Europe, Ireland has moved to the heart of European culture and policy-making. The mantra of independence that so much dominated political thinking for so many decades has given way now to interdependence as Michael Cronin outlines in 'Changing Times, Changing Cultures'. The willingness with which this huge change in political culture was accepted is an indication of the sophistication and truly multinational outlook of the Irish people. But just as Ireland has changed in thirty years of EU membership, so also has Europe changed, as Professor Cronin points out. And certainly change will continue as interdependence increases between the nations of the world, as communication and travel break down ever more barriers and as people become tolerant and appreciative of cultural differences rather than fearful. History tells us that the interaction of different cultures results in the exchange of the more attractive and beneficial features of each. Through the centuries Ireland and the European continent have been inseparable and cultural interchange has been the norm. Over our thirty-year membership of the EU, this exchange has been enhanced to encompass all aspects of our ways of life.

Economic Development

Those old enough to remember the seventies and eighties will know that the economic benefits that accrued to Ireland from EU membership did not become evident immediately. However, as Dr Garret FitzGerald demonstrates in 'The Economics of EU Membership', the benefits would eventually be greater than imagined by even the pro-membership groups who campaigned for membership in the early 1970s. The boost to agriculture, the transfer of regional funds and above all free access to wealthy European markets ensured that Ireland navigated the troubled seventies in far better condition than we could otherwise have hoped. Indeed, during the first ten years of membership, as Dr FitzGerald points out, the population of Ireland increased by 400,000, the first ever reversal of the emigrant culture that had plagued Ireland until then.

The Community was never going to be the exclusive panacea to Ireland's economic woes. Nor was it expected to be. The economic reforms and disciplines that eventually led to the enormous growth and prosperity of the Irish economy were the initial measures necessary to modernize the Irish economy. But it is equally true to say that membership of the Community was both a complement and a catalyst to such reforms in the first place. Nobody could seriously argue that the economic boom that lifted Ireland to estimated GDP per capita levels of 125 per cent of the European average in 2002 from 58 per cent in 1973 could have achieved such a result on its own. Perhaps it could have been achieved without membership, as Mr Hourihane describes, but with much more pain, much less support and on a much longer time-scale. The free access to European markets that came with membership of the Community not only opened the world's richest markets to Irish exporters but also ensured that Foreign Direct Investment would flow into Ireland from non-EU countries in order to avail of such market access.

Social Change

Too often the concept of economic reform raises the image of a deterioration in social conditions. In the case of Ireland, and the European Union, the opposite has proven to be the case. As David Begg shows in 'People, Work and Social Change', economic advancement was achieved side-by-side with the most far- reaching and progressive changes to social policy. The Taoiseach, Bertie Ahern, also makes this point in his lecture when he stresses that rather than joining a race to the bottom, standards were stabilized and raised across the Union. From the earliest introduction of equal pay in compliance with EU laws, which was spearheaded by Ireland's first Commissioner, Dr Patrick J. Hillery, through to the ongoing development of various social policies to protect workers' rights, to increased workers' benefits and the introduction of the Social Charter, Ireland and the Union provide an example of how economic progress can be achieved without the necessity to curtail advances in social policy.

The push towards competitiveness, especially in the context of globalization of markets, as Mr Begg rightly points out, can, in an uncontrolled environment, result in excesses that benefit the few to the detriment of the many. The Union has shown in the past that it is capable of acting to protect and enhance social as opposed to corporate interests. For example, in the area of consumer protection, the improved standards applied to manufacturing and processing industries and the introduction of stringent health protection regulations have helped to enhance confidence in the marketplace to the benefit of consumers and suppliers. Where co-operation is not always forthcoming from the vested interests affected, the Union has not shirked from acting. For example, the efforts that were necessary to curb tobacco advertising was a case where the Union acted in the interests of the general public in the face of fierce opposition from the tobacco industry and, indeed, a number of national governments.

Such determined opposition to sensible measures, however, is thankfully the exception. Many of the Union's greatest successes rest on its ability to work with all interested parties, national governments, regional authorities, industry and workers' representatives, consumer groups and NGOs to find a common ground to legislate for the benefit of all.

The Future
And as we look forward to the next thirty years of membership, already we can see a developing Union with the proposals emerging from the Intergovernmental Conference on the report of the Convention on the Future of Europe. Whatever shape the final treaty may take, it is clear that it will be governed by the principles that have stood the Union so well since its inception, and which the Taoiseach stresses in his contribution, namely

respect for national identities and the development of strong and efficient institutions to serve Europe. The argument in Dr Larry Siedentop's paper touches on the ideal out-turn — only when institutions lead people to put aside their own interests and preferences in order to consider instead what promotes or serves the common interest, does democracy work as it ought to. In essence that is what the European Union has striven to achieve in its short history and has done so with considerable success. It must remain our central aim for the future.

In conclusion, I would like to congratulate all of those involved in the production of these excellent lectures in the prestigious Thomas Davis series. The Commission, through its representation in Dublin, was pleased to be able to give its support to this timely venture as Ireland prepares to assume the Presidency of the EU for the first six months of 2004. Special credit is due to RTÉ and the many staff involved in the production, especially AnnMarie O'Callaghan who commissioned the series and Seamus Hosey who produced it. The contributors are to be commended for their thoughtful and provoking views. Mr Jim Hourihane of St Patrick's College, Drumcondra, deserves special thanks for the time that he has taken not only to devise and organize the lecture series but also to edit and publish this book of contributions. I am sure that it will remain a reference for students of EU affairs for many years.

Commissioner David Byrne

Introduction

In 1973, nobody could possibly have foreseen the Ireland of 2002. Physical sciences, based as they are on experimentation and precise measurement of results, can predict outcomes with a great degree of certainty. Social sciences, possessing a far greater number of unpredictable variables, can only make their best, informed guesses at what the future will be like. Ireland performed a massive leap of faith by joining the six founding states of the European Economic Community, in spite of what was described by one politician at the time as 'a future of unprecedented demand' for the agricultural produce that the Irish economy depended on so heavily at the time.

Ireland first applied for full membership in July 1961. Two significant difficulties caused reservations on the part of the existing members, especially France. Firstly, Ireland was economically underdeveloped. Secondly, its neutrality and non-membership of NATO was problematic. Ireland was also seen to be too closely linked, especially in economic terms, with Britain.

General de Gaulle, the President of France, first appeared to welcome an Irish membership, although it would not be full but rather associative in nature. But in January 1963 de Gaulle ended the negotiations between the EEC and Britain and de facto indefinitely postponed Ireland's negotiations with the EEC.

Ireland and Britain renewed their applications for membership in May 1967. On 3 November 1967, while hosting a lunch at the Elysée Palace for an Irish government delegation led by the Taoiseach, Jack Lynch, General de Gaulle said:

> For this Europe to be European, it must take into account the existence of the six continental states and it is of capital importance that this Community should reinforce itself and develop. It should include the association of other western states with the Community. It should also include détente, understanding and co-operation with the states in the centre and eastern parts of our continent. Everything indicates that Ireland can and should be closely associated with the accomplishment of this great work. [1]

His toast clearly offered only associative membership to Ireland, Britain, Norway and Denmark. General de Gaulle did not allow negotiations to begin again. Just three weeks after making this speech of support he stated that France was not prepared to enter into negotiations with Britain and the other applicant countries. So what sort of Community did he have in mind? It was certainly one that would not be threatened by British membership – viewed by the French as bringing a perceived element of American involvement in the affairs of Europe. 'Europe without Britain existed,' he declared, 'Europe without France was unthinkable.' His continental dimensions of Europeanism were central to his thinking. In his view the British were not really part of the European continent – they lived on an island. Being even farther removed from this continentality, and so closely linked in economic terms with Britain, Ireland was not going to be viewed any more favourably than Britain.

General de Gaulle's Europe stretched from the Atlantic to the Urals, the traditional physical boundary within the land mass of Eurasia. It was a Europe centred on the Low Countries, a Europe dominated by France. Any attempts to generate or cultivate unity within the diversity of the European states after the Second World War were never going to be easy. European states had much that united them but far more that divided them. Languages, social values, currencies, perspectives on the places they occupied in the European and world orders were always going to represent significant challenges to a wider unity.

How, therefore, did Ireland, a relatively small, insignificant state on the western edge of Europe, possess such self-belief that it was prepared, just four years after the formation of the EEC in 1957, to join with the six founding members? It may be explained at a number of levels. Most immediately, Ireland was attempting to join a Community whose dominant policy for many years after its formation was agriculture. The Common Agricultural Policy would provide expanded markets with prices far higher than those available more widely around the world. A second explanation may be found in Ireland's growing confidence and outward-looking view of itself as articulated in T.K. Whitaker's *Report on Economic Development* of the late 1950s. This growth in self-belief and outward-looking view also lay in the Treaty of Rome that formed the EEC in 1957. There are 248 articles in the Treaty. In essence it comprised four freedoms: freedom of movement for goods, people, services and capital. Ireland was not in the early 1960s a service or capital-rich country. Its people had for long been projected into an unfree movement – that of emigration. Freedom of movement of goods represented a huge attraction, especially, as already mentioned, in the agriculture area.

A further reason for Ireland looking towards Europe lay in the nature of its spatial relations, both within Ireland and with the wider world. Statehood had been achieved in 1922 and there was an inevitable movement onwards and outwards in its spatial settings as time progressed. The French philosopher, Henri Lefebvre, argued that 'as the product, the child, of a space, the state turns back toward its own historical conditions and antecedents, and transforms them'.

Elaborating on this set of relations Lefebvre saw the defining moments as:

> Firstly, the production of a space, the national terri-
> tory, a physical space, mapped, modified and transformed.
>
> Secondly, the production of a social space based on
> hierarchically ordered institutions, of laws and conven-
> tions upheld by values.
>
> Thirdly, the production of a mental space that includes
> the representations of the state that people construct –
> confused or clear, directly experienced or conceptually
> elaborated. [2]

If looked at from this conceptual perspective one may argue that the national territory had been established in 1922. The second layer of space, the social, based on institutions, was properly in place and had been reinforced by the passage of time. There remained, therefore, only the third layer of space: the mental. This was to be put in place by Ireland's growing self-assuredness, its outward-looking vision of itself and, I would suggest, by its membership of the then EEC in 1973 and, subsequently, the EC and EU.

The eight essays that form this book were broadcast as a Thomas Davis lecture series on RTÉ in late 2002 and early 2003. They helped mark the thirtieth anniversary of Ireland's membership of the European Union. My own lecture, 'The Dynamics of Membership', places Ireland's membership within a spatial framework that has evolved since 1922 but also finds its roots in the interaction of environment, people and politics. Professor Michael Cronin examines the changing nature of Irish culture within a broader European and globalized context. Cathryn Costello assesses the impact of European Union membership on Irish law and posits the changing nature of Irish law within this framework. David Begg analyses the impact of thirty years of Ireland's membership on people, work and broader social change. Professor Brigid Laffan examines the interrelationship between Irish and European politics. Dr Garret FitzGerald assesses the economic impact of membership and the development of the Irish economy over the thirty-year period. Dr Larry Siedentop places Irish membership within the broader realm of the search for the most democratic structures of European identity and belonging. Taoiseach Bertie Ahern's essay on Ireland's capacity and ability to embrace change over the years of membership emphasizes the growth and development of Ireland and its people in a wider European framework.

The European Union is about to enlarge its membership from the current fifteen member states by an additional ten in mid-2004. Apart from assessing Ireland's first thirty years of membership of the EU, these essays also indicate how Ireland successfully adapted its economy and culture within the European Union. From this perspective it may well function as a model for at least some of the incoming member states in 2004 – especially those whose geographic advantages and restrictions, levels of economic development, sizes and populations approximate those of Ireland when we joined the EU.

The European Union has transformed the economic, political and social architecture of today's Ireland. To suggest otherwise would be to deny the reality of a modern, multicultural and assured country and its people.

Ireland *and the* European Union

The First Thirty Years, 1973–2002

1. The Dynamics of Membership

Jim Hourihane

Europe can be quite confusing. Geographers accept that Europe is one of the continents but it's quite unlike other continents such as Africa, and North and South America. Those all possess a quality that is generally regarded as basic to continentality – physical separation from other large landmasses.

Europe is the western portion of the much larger landmass of Eurasia. Yet Europe's continental status is very real. It doesn't lie in physical separation from Asia. We find it instead in the people who live there. These people and their ancestors have modified and constructed their environments and landscapes over time within the space we refer to as Europe. European people have adapted and evolved through many centuries to where they now have their own frameworks of social and economic structures.

There's another way in which the word Europe is used, in the growing tendency to refer to the fifteen member states of the European Union as Europe. It's clearly effective as a shorthand way of referring to the European Union but it assumes that the

European Union is Europe. It's not. Until such time as the forty or so countries that form the continent of Europe are all members of the European Union there should not be an interchange-ability of these two different uses of the word Europe.

In December 2002, we were at a point in time where two quite significant anniversaries occurred. Eighty years earlier, on 6 December 1922, the Irish State was founded. The other anniversary occurred on 31 December, when the thirtieth year of our European Union membership came to a close.

Napoleon's comment that 'the policy of a state lies in its geography' was true of Ireland at many levels in 1922. It became less true in 1973 when we joined the European Community, and it's even less true now. When one of Mikhail Gorbachev's spokesmen was asked what the difference was between the fall of the Berlin Wall in 1989 and the invasion of Czechoslovakia in 1968, he thought for a second, then replied, 'About twenty years.' In just the same way, the differences between the Ireland of 1922, 1973 and 2002 are also not only differences in time but in the very architecture of our lives, our landscapes and our minds. Many of these differences over the last thirty years, I would suggest, have been defined to a significant degree by our membership of the European Union.

Shakespeare's Hamlet caught the concept of spatial boundaries succinctly: 'O God! I could be bounded in a nut-shell, and count myself a king of infinite space, were it not that I have bad dreams.' While we had succeeded in establishing a state in 1922, we had reason to have at least some bad dreams. Although we had secured our independence from Britain, the legacy of a long colonial oppression was not easily eradicated. We were geographically proximate, so any likely future external trade – especially given the nature of transportation at the time – would, in all probability, be with Britain.

The spaces occupied by states are clearly unequal and our national space compared with that of the British empire in 1922 was unequal. As a minor power, we focused initially on agricultural development – the aspect of our economy that made the European Community so appealing when we first joined. There were good reasons for concentration on agriculture – memories of the Great Famine were still part of the Irish folk memory. Robert Malthus, the English economist, wrote in 1817 that the land of Ireland 'is infinitely more peopled than in England; and to give full effect to the natural resources of the country, a great part of the population should be swept from the soil'.[1] He changed his mind later, somewhat conditionally, suggesting that if enough capital was expended on Irish economic development, its carrying capacity would increase. The Great Famine of the 1840s was to do in one sweep what he had spoken of thirty years earlier: directly in the one million or so deaths it caused and indirectly by greatly increasing the existing pattern of emigration. The large population of Ireland in the mid-nineteenth century was rurally based, and this structural orientation towards land wasn't to be lessened for another full century.

Lack of capital, natural resources and human resources have also been assessed by historians and economists as further reasons why Ireland was so agriculturally dependent at the time of independence. Whatever the relative weighting of any of these factors in explaining why Ireland did not follow the European model of development, we were still geographically and economically very much linked to Britain.

The policy of economic self-sufficiency of the 1930s was accompanied by the introduction of widespread tariffs. Most Western European countries saw them as a way of protecting their own economies during the Depression and that legacy didn't easily disappear.

From Ireland's viewpoint, tariffs made us very inward look-ing. Only in the late 1950s were radical economic steps articu-lated – ones that looked at a fuller picture in both the structure of the economy and the possibility of engaging wider geographic frameworks. T.K. Whitaker's *Report on Economic Development* characterized Irish agriculture as backward and identified the lack of industry as a major issue that needed to be addressed by the government.

The creation of a Common Market under the Treaty of Rome in 1957 clearly pointed the way forward for Ireland. Taoiseach Seán Lemass oversaw the dismantling of the trade barriers that he had so advocated as a minister in the 1930s. Tearing down these protectionist barriers showed a new confidence and a new dynamism.

The need to move towards free trade and a freer world was captured by the American poet, Robert Frost in his 1914 poem 'Mending Wall':

> My apple trees will never get across
> And eat the cones under his pines, I tell him.
> He only says 'good fences make good neighbours'.

Good fences don't make for good neighbours in terms of trade. As would be seen subsequently within the European Commu-nity, the free movement of capital, ideas, goods and services across national borders ideally suited a country such as Ireland.

When Ireland first applied for membership of the European Community on 31 July 1961 it met with both mixed signals and strong reservations. Italy, Germany and the Benelux countries appeared to accept the assurances offered by the Irish political leaders and diplomats about our economic prospects and our attitudes towards the fact that the existing six members of the Community were also members of NATO.

General de Gaulle as President of France had profound reservations. He emphasized the continental nature of the six existing member states. While accepting that the community would reinforce itself and develop, he saw incoming member states in an associative light rather than that of full membership. His choice of the French word *détente* to describe future understanding and co-operation with the states of the central and eastern parts of Europe was value-laden. It was a reflection of French dominance in defining the future development of Europe, especially in the central buffer zone – the old Mitteleuropa – between West and East.

He rejected the 1961–2 applications for membership by Ireland, Britain, Denmark and Norway. In 1967 he would not allow negotiations to begin. He was clearly determined that Jung's 1930 suggestion that 'Europe is dangerously close to becoming a mere hyphen between America and Asia' would not come to pass. There were concerns about Ireland's fitness for membership from an economic perspective but the main difficulty lay in geo-politics and Ireland's neutrality, our non-membership of NATO as well as our overly close trading links with Britain.

By 1967, when Ireland attempted to renew its application for EEC membership, its trade links with Britain had become even firmer under the Anglo-Irish Free Trade Agreement that had been signed in 1965. This trade dependency, for that was what it was, had been recognized by Taoiseach Jack Lynch as far back as the 1950s when the Treaty of Rome was signed. Later, he was to speak about the 1957 Treaty:

> We did say at that time, that insofar as our interests lay in Europe, they lay with the countries then forming the European Economic Community, and that the most desirable arrangement for us would be a common market in which we would be members with Britain.[2]

France again rejected this second application for membership in November 1967 – de Gaulle simply threatened to veto. In 1969 George Pompidou succeeded General de Gaulle as President of France and promised not to block British and Irish membership. Negotiations began in 1970. They were concluded in 1971 and the 1972 Treaty of Accession led to Irish membership on 1 January 1973. In the referendum on membership in May 1972, 83 per cent of Irish voters supported it.

So why did Ireland join the European Community and what have the actual, as opposed to the prospective, dynamics of membership been like? At its simplest level, integration is the act of making parts into a unit. Geographically, it's a process by which the national borders – or the fences in Robert Frost's poem – are broken down within Europe – both formally and informally.

In this respect, our engagement of the dynamics of membership has reflected where the European Union came from. It was certainly called the European Economic Community during the early years of its existence but, in reality, it was founded because of the possibilities that were offered by an organization that was politically based and fully integrated, and would lessen the occurrence of further war within Western Europe.

There was a clear recognition of what John Updike described as 'time passing in America and Asia while in Europe history occurs'. The founders of the European Coal and Steel Community and, subsequently, the European Economic Community were determined that the history of the First and Second World Wars would not be repeated.

As a block, Europe is not as resource-rich as other regions of the world and it is logical to maximize the benefits available from extensive trading links inside and outside the Union. Such a philosophy could only appeal to a country like Ireland. It now has a very open economy and its engagement of the possibilities offered within the Union has been considerable on a number of levels.

The initial focus after our joining in 1973 was on agriculture, but subsequent spending reforms within the Union have proven to be similarly advantageous to Ireland. It could be argued that the heavy spending commitment to the Common Agricultural Policy in our early years of membership did not facilitate alternative and additional economic development within Ireland.

Subsequently, far greater levels of regional and structural funding helped us put ourselves in a position where we are capable of maximizing the growth of the Irish economy – especially in the technology sector during the 1990s.

The Spanish philosopher Ortega y Gasset in *The Revolt of the Masses* (1930) suggested that humankind's technological development falls broadly into three categories:

> The technology of chance
> The technology of handicraft
> And the technology of the technician

I'd suggest that Ireland's development over the last decade has shifted Ortega y Gasset's third category on towards a redefined technology of the technician: that of the technology of the informationalist, the globalist and the communicator.

Ireland's success in attracting foreign investment has been the source of not a little jealousy and of attempts to restrict our attractiveness by other member states, operating in what they term 'broader community interests'. The coincidence of community interests with national expectations is often very close!

The continent of Europe and the European Union have often been compared to an apple. At the core are the more economically developed and industrially advanced countries such as France, Germany and Benelux (Belgium, The Netherlands and Luxembourg). Countries such as Ireland have traditionally been viewed as forming the periphery or skin of the apple; not least of their problems was geographic removal from the central area where strong markets and a long history of industrialization existed.

Over time, of course, many of those older industries suffered from an inability to restructure as well as competition from outside the Union. It might be suggested that Ireland was spared the worst excesses of industrial change because we had relatively little industry to be changed.

Geographers might not go quite as far as auctioneers when saying that the three most important factors influencing development are location, location, location, but they certainly recognize its importance in promoting or retarding economic development.

Ireland struggled in this regard in its initial years of membership but in recent years has turned the disadvantage of location completely on its head. Its absolute location remains the same, but its relative location has changed hugely. The revolution in information and communication technology, so instrumental in the 1990s in helping birth the 'Celtic Tiger', proved that location had lost much of its geographic relevance when it came to new forms of industry like financial services.

The relative importance of globalization and Europeanization in our development over the last decade is impossible to determine with any certainty. Both are so interrelated they have sometimes completely coincided. American investment in Ireland has been a major source of economic development but, even allowing for Irish-American interests, would as much of that investment have occurred here if we were not members of the EU?

It is important to look at place and people as they have affected and have been affected by the dynamics of EU membership. From a geographical perspective, place has changed substantially in Ireland. The environment we've created is the result of space and time interacting and being influenced by the involvement of people and policies.

What sort of a place has Ireland become since 1973? Most obviously it is more urbanized as more and more people have moved out of agricultural employment, changing both the rural and urban landscapes. Traditionally, Irish people who left the countryside to migrate to towns and cities went on to urban areas outside Ireland. Since 1973, rural-urban migration has continued but many people have been afforded the opportunity to remain within the country.

There is also, now, a counter-urbanization happening and this presents us with a paradox. More and more Irish urbanization is in fact counter-urbanization and it's rural in nature – manifest in the one-off homes that are being built on the Irish rural land-scape. In part it's a product of the escalating costs of building or buying in Dublin and other population centres; a pattern that is likely to continue for some time.

There's the accompanying pressure on Dublin and Leinster as home to over half the current Irish population. If the recently announced National Spatial Strategy gets the funding it needs to succeed, it may change our serious regional imbalances.

One senses at times a mixed reaction in those who, with almost the same breath, rejoice in the way that 'place' has changed for the better in Ireland and yet bemoan the accompanying sense of loss of what has disappeared. We are more Euro-peanized in our shops, our foods and, not least, in our drinks. We have also become more speedy in how we approach life and less inclined to stand still and smell the roses. This gallop towards modernity isn't entirely due to Europeanization, but each partakes of the other.

How have Irish people changed over the last thirty years? For one thing, there are more of us living in Ireland. The recently published 2002 census figures show there are just under a million more people in the Republic than there were in 1971.

While the growth in population has been more or less continuous since joining the EU, two periods stand out. The first decade of EU membership saw our population grow by just under half a million, while 1996–2002 showed a population increase of just under 300,000 people.

The first phase of growth was largely triggered by natural increase rather than by in-migration, while the recent phase was more or less evenly caused by natural increase and net in-migration. Both phases are noteworthy, but for quite different reasons.

Back in the 1970s we still had very high birth rates that were well above European averages. Now, our birth rates have declined but our attractiveness as a destination for many types of migrants – returned emigrants, migrant workers, refugees and asylum seekers – has increased dramatically. One of our most significant developments since we joined the EU in 1973 has been the ability of our young Irish people to stay here and enjoy a much higher standard of living than might ever have been dreamed possible then, much less in 1922.

Jonathan Haughton has written about the lack of entrepreneurs throughout our early industrialization and the accompanying issue of endogeneity. Did entrepreneurs lead development or did they spring up when opportunities arose? The same problem arises in assessing the last thirty years, but the assuredness and confidence with which the younger generation enters the world of work and entrepreneurial opportunity is striking. There's a new occupational mobility, which, from the perspective of those in previous generations who were taught to believe that a good job was for life, is impossible to relate to. People are as fluid in terms of their attachment to specific jobs as they are to particular places.

The advent of ten new member states to the Union within the next few years is also a good reason for us to assess thirty years of membership. It does no harm for any society to look at where it's coming from and to gauge, at the same time, where it's going.

As we enlarge the European Union we will provide additional stimulus to the EU economies and counter any possible drift towards stagnation. We will also approach the spatial coverage outlined by Mikhail Gorbachev in his famous 1989 speech as the 'common European home'. He spoke of creating a 'European legal space' in which there would be 'complete uniformity in the understanding and application by all states of the norms of international law'. He went on to say, 'We envision Europe as a commonwealth of sovereign states with a high level of equitable interdependence and easily accessible borders, open to the exchange of products, technologies and ideas, and wide-ranging contacts among peoples.'

A comment made in late 2002 by a newspaper columnist from one of these incoming states struck me forcibly. It made the point that sovereignty was of little use if it only existed within the framework of one's own national borders. Sovereignty mattered more, according to the writer, if it was engaged within a broader spatial context such as the European Union. There's an inevitable logic in the movement from statehood to integration, and Ireland has provided a political template for such an aspiration.

We've also proven to many analysts that the deficiencies of geography as much as the vagaries of history can be overcome. While we may well have reached where we are today without membership of the European Union, we would not have done it as quickly or as painlessly without the support of our fellow member states.

2. Changing Times, Changing Cultures

Michael Cronin

In 1952 Evans Brothers in London published a work on Ireland by Geoffrey Taylor that was somewhat unadventurously titled *The Emerald Isle*. It was part of a series called 'Windows on the World' and the book itself was in part a personal essay and in part a travel account. Taylor, himself an Irishman, begins the final chapter on 'Ireland To-Day' with the following unambiguous statement: 'In an age in which most countries are increasingly conscious of their interdependence – displaying almost a desperate desire to hang together – Ireland is perhaps uniquely isolationist.'[1] The half-century that has elapsed since Taylor's verdict has seen a dramatic change in Ireland's social, economic and cultural circumstances.

The uniqueness of Ireland's isolation in Taylor's proud boast has now given way to the uniqueness of Ireland's interdependence. Ireland is now fully integrated into the global market economy. The country has been a member state of the European Union since 1973 and it currently holds a seat on the United Nations Security Council. If the minting of a new Irish coinage in 1928 was a highly symbolic moment of national independence, the adoption of the Euro in 2001 was an eloquent illustration of national interdependence. This essay will explore how Irish culture has been affected by the political and economic developments of recent decades and, in particular, to what extent a European dimension has featured in the transformations of Irish culture.

Ireland's geographic isolation as an island nation fed many myths about the country, but the problem was that for many decades after independence, it fed few mouths. In the 1970s, however, a significant change would take place in the way the developed world did business, with telecommunications and informatics allowing for manufacturing activities and the provision of services to be shifted away from traditional, congested, high-cost centres of production. This is part of what the French thinker Paul Virilio calls the shift from geo-politics to chrono-politics in modernity.[2] In his view, it is the positioning of countries in technologically constructed time-zones rather than immutable physical landscapes or fixed territorial space that determines their military, economic and cultural fortunes. If peripherality was a constant in Irish political and economic thinking in the 1970s, the very notion itself was being undermined by infrastructural investment in telecommunications in the 1980s where the basis was laid for the new network-based economy. In this new economy, based on telecommunications and computer networks, it is the state, accessibility and extent of the networks that are important, not Ireland's physical location off the western seaboard of mainland Europe. In a sense, Ireland's physical periphery has transformed itself into a 'virtual centre' in areas such as hi-tech manufacturing, international financial services, software translation, teleservices and pharmaceuticals. It really is no longer a question of ourselves alone but ourselves online.

Connection/Disconnection

The new virtual geography of the island brings us to the first decisive shift in Irish culture and this revolves around connectedness and disconnectedness. In 1949 there were only 43,000 exchange lines in Ireland. Only a third of these were residential. A phone in the hallway was as rare as a car in the driveway. At the time an Irish person made an average of one call every fortnight. In 1997 there were 1,427,000 exchange lines and the total number of calls made was nearly eight billion. Already in 1996, on average, every man, woman and child in Ireland was making (and receiving) around six calls a day.[3] The country now has one of the highest rates of mobile phone usage in the world. As a nation we cannot stop talking to each other and the telecommunications revolution with the digitalization of the trunk transmission network in the eighties means that the opportunities to do so are now almost unlimited. Thus, the advent of new technology means on the face of it that we have entered a paradise of connectedness. Internet usage, although still largely determined by class and income, has brought information, services and correspondents, both at home and abroad, much closer. Phone calls, text messages and e-mails make the island a veritable hive of language, with countless connections established every second. We are no longer unique in the EU in our telephonic isolation. We are now models of communicative interdependence.

If we are now connected more than we ever have been before where does disconnectedness come from? Where and when, in other words, do our connections break down? To answer this question we need to consider the impact of historical European notions of the self. An important moment in the development of a certain kind of European modernity, which begins with the

Renaissance and the Reformation and reaches its culminating point in the French Revolution, is the emergence of the individual. No longer the powerless subject of church, monarchy and tradition, the individual seeks emancipation from inherited dogma and political tyranny and seeks to freely fashion his or her own life. The economic version of this ideal is the independent agent who seeks to maximize opportunities for profit on the free market with other similarly emancipated agents. Modernity is presented as the inexorable movement towards the birth of the fully sovereign individual. A major part of the story that Ireland has been telling itself over the last thirty years is a parable of modernization as a triumph of individual will. In the dark days of the pre-modern, Ireland was beholden to the twin forces of Faith and Fatherland. Individual freedoms were severely restricted and many of the classics of European literature fell foul of the censor. On the economic front, the country was steadily impoverished by trade tariffs, misguided import-substitution policies and limits on foreign direct capital investment. Leaving aside the element of caricature in the account, this was obviously no country for freethinkers or free marketeers. As the critic Joe Cleary has pointed out, 'In the Irish context there is a particularly acute stress on modernization not simply as a matter of technological or industrial development, but as a project which is expected to deliver cultural and psychological enlightenment as well.'[4] This makes Irish motives for choosing Europe different from those of other countries. The collective ideal of putting an end to military conflict was not one of the attractions of Europe for Ireland. The Irish, after all, had not been party to the Second World War – the event that had deeply affected the founding fathers of the European project and led them to lay the basis for the Union. Rather, what made Europe desirable was the older European ideal of autonomous individuals, makers of their own political, economic and cultural destinies. The rights of Irish individuals to equal pay or freedom from State harassment as a result of sexual orientation could now be vindicated in a European setting with its long-standing commitment to the autonomy of the individual. Privatization, deregulation and free trade were adopted as core elements of EU economic policy and were seen to be part of the liberation of the individual as an economic agent. What has followed has been the individualization of everything from tax regimes to convenience food in supermarkets.

No area of our culture has been untouched by this development. The trend is even noticeable in our choice of places to live. The average household size fell continuously between 1946 and 1996 and the number of one-person households has more than trebled since 1946. So, the period which has seen the technical potential for connectedness increase exponentially, has also witnessed the growing disconnectedness of people. That is to say, the Irish are less likely to see themselves as a group sharing a set of inherited collective ideals than as a collection of individuals, each person with their own set of goals and objectives. The fact that Irish society has shifted from a rural to an urban base has further accelerated this movement towards the privatization of experience. At the end of the 1940s only 20 per cent lived in towns of more than 1500 people. Now the figure is over 60 per cent and rising.[5] This is, doubtless, one of the reasons for the complaints by visitors about what they perceive as the growing coldness or indifference of the Irish.

The decisive shift from the collective self to the individual self means a greater wariness about contact with others as each contact must be negotiated individually rather than collectively. The wariness also explains the considerable emphasis on crime and punishment in contemporary Irish culture. This is not only because statistically there is more crime than there used to be but because in an increasingly disconnected society, we feel we can never quite be sure of the intentions of the stranger that we meet. Contact is seen more and more as a risky business. By a curious paradox, the instruments of our connectedness have become the means of our disconnectedness. The cars that bring people to their friends at the end of the journey prevent them from befriending anybody on the way. Indeed, one of the tasks of Irish urban planners in recent years has been to try and reclaim the collective, public space of the city from the individual, private needs of the car. The aim has been to make the city a dwelling place as opposed to a transit zone, a place where people can meet up rather than be knocked down. In a similar way, television has brought Ireland and the world into people's living rooms and connected them to the news of each other through the small screen. However, a screen that reveals can also be a screen that conceals or hides. The viewer is concealed not only from those present on the screen but from the hundreds of thousands of others watching the same screen. Hence, the decline of social activities that must compete against the comfort factor of the zapper, the multiplication of channels making even the shared reference of popular programmes (such as 'The Late, Late Show' in its heyday) increasingly rare.

It is possible to argue that what Irish culture has experienced over the last three decades is an individualizing tendency, which is both European and American in origin. The European origin lies in European philosophical and political experience that gave rise to the Enlightenment and a conceptual framework for European law, which will affect all areas of Irish life. The American origin has to do with a strong commitment to individualism in American neo-liberalism and the influence of US values on globalization, both economic and cultural. As over 75 per cent of all foreign direct investment in Ireland over the last decade has come from US-based companies, the incorporation of Ireland into global US business policy is inevitable. One of the difficulties in trying to determine what factors are responsible for cultural change in Ireland is that both the United States and the European Union are party to the project of globalization. Indeed, the most decisive shift in the history of the European Union has been the move from an organization designed to end war in Europe to an organization primarily concerned with defending Europe's economic interests in the global economy. If Ireland has changed much in the last thirty years, so too has the European Union and the relationship is not one between a dynamic mover and a static monolith but one between two shifting entities.

Mobility

There has, of course, been much dynamic movement. One of the paradoxes of late modernity is that the more we invent technologies like the Internet and videoconferencing that would seem to dispense with the need to travel, the more we travel. The Irish are a case in point. In the eight years from 1986 to 1994, growth in the number of air passengers on the Dublin-London route was twice that of any other European route from the UK.[6] In 1999 the number of Irish visitors going abroad was just over 3.5 million compared with 2.5 million in 1996 – an increase of around one million in a relatively short three-year period. Travel is as much a matter of return as of departure. No country or its culture is left untouched by the return of the native population. When tourists return from their holidays they not only bring back snapshots but they carry with them memories of the food they ate, the wine they drank, the clothes they wore. And it is these experiences they want to prolong or relive in going out to a restaurant or having pasta for lunch or French cheese with their dinner or a bottle of Spanish wine in a nightclub. In this way, the conventional distinction between domestic and foreign cultures begins to break down as everything from the shelves in supermarkets to T-shirts at the bus stop shows the influence of an increasingly nomadic population. Dwelling and travelling no longer seem like such polar opposites. The Irish not only travel more in travelling but also in their dwelling as they continue their travels through the cultures of Europe and farther afield.

The new tourists are not the first to travel to Europe, and Irish cultural modernism has a distinguished list of European exiles. One of those, James Joyce, begins *Ulysses* with a description of the shaving glass that Buck Mulligan offers to him as the 'cracked lookingglass of a servant', a suitable symbol he feels for Irish art.[7] It might have been the symbol for any area of Irish culture. In view of Ireland's centuries-old and often difficult relationship with her island neighbour, the Anglo-Irish mirror did on occasion prove to be a dispiriting distortion. Entry into the European Union meant that the terms of Irish self-perception and self-expression would not always be dictated by an overly familiar binary relationship with its inevitable sets of presuppositions and prejudices. This meant in turn that the Anglo-Irish relationship itself could be looked at anew, as it was in negotiations leading to the Good Friday agreement. Ireland's European experiences provided the confidence for a more fruitful engagement with the British dimension to Irish life. Furthermore, it was in the context of a Europe of nations and regions that it made perfect political and cultural sense to engage more effectively with Scotland and Wales, even if much still remains to be done.

Instantaneous Time/Durational Time

If we see ourselves differently thirty years into EU membership, how do we now live in our present and what have we decided to do with our past? In this context, it may be useful to return to our changing material circumstances. It is commonly argued that different modes of production are defined by what is needed to increase productivity. In the agricultural mode of development, increasing surplus comes from increases in the amount of labour or natural resources such as land that are available for the production process. New energy sources like steam and electricity are the principal source of productivity in the industrial mode of development, alongside the ability to distribute energy through appropriate circulation and production processes. In the informational mode of development, the shift is from a technology based primarily on cheap inputs of energy to one predominantly based on cheap inputs of information derived from advances in micro-electronic and telecommunications technology.[8] Rapid access to information allows us to respond more quickly to and even anticipate change whether in fashion or high finance. The comparative advantage of small nations, therefore, is to take the waiting out of wanting. As the old telecommunications advertisement goes, stand still and you're history.

The speeding up of Irish life is evident in the death gullies of our roads and also in the frenzied multi-tasking of the average working life. The silent solemnity of Sundays is a thing of the past as the convenience stores and shopping centres bring us closer to the so-called 24/7 culture – a non-stop, 24-hour-day, 7-day-week culture of consumption. This is the world of instantaneous time. It is one of the time-zones inhabited by Ireland in the contemporary world, a time-zone that we use as a benchmark of our progress from the sluggish pieties of the grey years of austerity.

Our culture has also generated a longing for another kind of time that we might call durational time. Durational time is time that lasts. It is time considered over a long period and which is consequently valued because it reminds us of earlier periods. There are two areas where we can see this durational time coming to the fore. The first is in the area of family history where there has been an exponential growth in genealogy in recent years. Decades ago 'roots tourism' brought Americans to our shores in search of their ancestors but now it is the native Irish themselves who, in a rootless modernity, are looking for affinities with the past. The second area where durational time takes pride of place is the heritage industry. In the past thirty years in Ireland, there has been a very marked increase in the number of heritage-based attractions in the country. These include historic houses and castles, interpretive centres, museums and folk parks, nature and wildlife parks, historic monuments and heritage gardens.[9] It is easy to see their development as cynical opportunism on the part of the tourism industry but this would be to ignore the fact that a great many heritage-based attractions are visited not so much by foreign nationals as by Irish locals. What the attractions offer is a contact with another experience of place and more particularly, another sense of time, captured in landscape or stone. Increasingly then, our culture is caught between two time-zones, the double-quick zone of instantaneous time and the slow-running zone of durational time. The difficulty in both our private and political lives in Ireland is to create a culture that will accommodate both possibilities of living in late modernity.

The Jogging Effect

How we view any stretch of time depends of course on where we now stand and how things are. We would not offer the same interpretation of the Irish past if we were speaking in the depressed 1980s compared to the buoyant 1990s. Nor do people react to times past in the same way. For some, there is a bitter truth in the Swedish proverb that everyone over the age of fifty becomes a foreigner in their own country. The place they have grown up in has become unrecognizable, a cold, alien place where they no longer feel at home. For others, the present is a welcome redemption from the dark past of Faith and Fatherland. As the society becomes more multi-ethnic and less culturally homogenous, it feels more like the home they want to live in. These oppositions are, perhaps, too easy and we need to take a more nuanced view of what has happened and what is happening to us. One of the difficulties we have in analysing our condition is that we tend to confuse technical time and historical time. By this, I mean that we often tend to present time as a continuous, linear and irreversible process, that what has happened before will never be repeated again and that what is past is definitely and truly past. The time of the scientist is not however the time of the historian or the social commentator. To give an example, the arrival and subsequent spread of the motor car led to dire predictions everywhere of the wasting away of our lower limbs so that in due evolutionary course, legs would wither away and wheels take over. What has happened instead is that our towns, cities and countryside are filled with panting, perspiring humans determined to push their legs to their physical limits. Exhaustion rather than extinction is the order of the day. What has been called the 'jogging effect' shows that it is a mistake to project irreversible technical time onto human and social time, which culturally speaking knows no such irreversibility.[10] We do not go from the present into the future systematically dispensing with everything from the past but we keep on returning to those elements of the past that we find attractive or useful.

In Ireland during the last thirty years of EU membership the Irish language, which had been held up by some as the symbol of the sow that ate her dissenting farrow, has in fact flourished in the new broadcast media. Though the language is still under great pressure territorially in the Gaeltacht, it is part of an Irish past that has been dramatically reinvented in the Irish present in everything from primary-level schooling to third-level Masters courses in computing and high finance. Similarly, the urban renewal programmes in Dublin, Cork, Galway and Limerick and the conservation projects in Irish towns and villages show that as we progress further into the future, we are increasingly anxious to salvage the past. From the revival of figure- and step-dancing to the vogue for indigenous materials in clothing and construction, the past is not so much another country as part of the other country we are trying to build. Though it's easy to mock the more manipulative uses of historical memory, as in for example, the heritage booze barns that have appeared in many of our towns and cities, it is important to note how Irish society has had a complex and by no means predictable relationship with its own past.

The Risk Society

It is estimated that Ireland is now four times wealthier than it was at the moment of independence.[11] This wealth is not, of course, distributed equally throughout Irish society and income inequalities have grown consistently over the last three decades.[12] However, even for those enjoying a moderate level of prosperity, material well-being has not always meant peace of mind. Theft, burglary, and in particular, violent assault, if still relatively low by European standards, feature prominently in our newspapers and on our television screens. If the sign on many exits in department stores and supermarkets states, 'This door is alarmed,' then it seems that so also are we as a people. Going out at night becomes an elaborate risk management exercise and trust gives way to fearfulness as we transfer the advice given to children – 'Don't talk to strangers' – into our adult lives. This sense of fretfulness does not simply relate to our physical safety on the streets or in our homes. It also has to do with a greater anxiety about the environment in which we live. A feature of European Union involvement in Ireland since membership has been EU prominence in the area of the environment. Through a series of regulations, the EU has sought to protect the environment against developments that are actually or potentially harmful. What the ecological reawakening of the 1970s brought was a realization that the planet was not a disposable object. When NASA astronauts showed us the earth on their horizon, we gradually became aware that it was the only home we had. We did not have any other homes to go to if we made this one uninhabitable. Ireland, like many other European countries, has become a risk society.[13] From what we do with our waste to what we put on our plates, we have become more and more concerned with how to control the risks in our environment and our lives. Much of our attention indeed has become focused on how to deal with the risks that have been generated by prosperity – a prosperity that is often justified in terms of ending the classic Irish risks of poverty and displacement through emigration.

Irish emigration has now become European immigration and it is often forgotten that immigrants from the European Union have been arriving into Ireland consistently since 1973, though in greater numbers in recent years. The thousands of French, German, Dutch, Italian and Spanish citizens, to mention only a few groups, living, working and studying in Ireland have played their part in shaping the new Ireland. The challenge for Irish society is to make a virtue not of isolation but of interdependence and to ensure that our uniqueness lies in our continued need for others. It may indeed be the sum of our debts that constitutes our true wealth as a people.

3. Irish and European Law

Cathryn Costello

European Union law is all around us. It's vast in terms of the range of activities it covers and deep in terms of its impact. For example, when challenging the planning permission for the O'Connell Street Spire, the Environmental Impact Assessment Directive was invoked.[1] When concerned citizens sought to prevent Monsanto trials of genetically modified seeds, another European directive was relied upon.[2] Milk quota litigation sagas are common in the Irish courts.[3] Gender equality law in Ireland – in the workplace and in social security – is entirely a consequence of Ireland's European Union membership.[4] Other types of discrimination such as those based on race, disability, age and sexual orientation became subject to EU law more recently.[5] Market opening and regulatory measures are all governed by EU law – be it mobile phone licensing or aviation regulation.[6]

There is no denying the pervasive effects of the EU. EU law is clearly not 'out there' – it is part of the Irish domestic legal system and indeed, estimates suggest that 60 per cent of all our domestic laws are of European origin. This state of affairs is often underrepresented. Dashwood has memorably described this: 'The individual citizen ... continues to experience government as essentially a Member State phenomenon. Rules touching the lives of individuals in all kinds of ways may no longer be home-produced; but the consequences of the rules are exacted by officials with familiar accents and uniforms.'[7]

What I aim to do in this essay is throw some light on three things: I want to talk about the nature of European law, and how it has come that its application of Community law at the domestic level is now routine, even unremarkable. This process I will describe is the 'constitutionalization' of European law. Secondly, I want to examine the processes of making EU law and their shortcomings. Finally, I want to look at some of the current debates – which seek at once to address some of the legitimacy deficits in the EU and to formalize the constitutional developments that have taken place.

This is a momentous period in EU development. Grandiose constitutional designs for the EU are being developed at a feverish pace. The Convention on the Future of Europe has prepared a draft Constitutional Treaty for the EU. The Intergovernmental Conference that led to the Treaty of Nice was fractious and protracted, leading to the realization that the classic method of EU Treaty change was inadequate. Hence, the Convention was convened in March 2002 to provide an open deliberative forum in which to reach a constitutional settlement for the EU. Having prepared the draft Constitutional Treaty, it now falls to another Intergovernmental Conference, convened in October 2003, to finalize the bargain. A legal analysis of the EU is a prerequisite to engagement in the current debates, particularly as we simultaneously attempt to assess thirty years of membership.

In Ireland, some commentators express surprise at the absence

of engagement with the EU in light of this series of popular referenda. Aside from the lamentable tenor of those debates pre-
Nice II, it must be borne in mind that the Treaties establish
broad legislative powers for the institutions. Periodic popular
ratification of the general framework is no replacement for the
proper accountability of the legislative organs. Nonetheless, the
debate surrounding the second Nice referendum was welcome
in its frankness and accuracy. However, I would characterize this
debate as one of 'catching-up' with current practices.

The incremental nature of EU Treaty change over the past
two decades has made each individual Treaty difficult to explain
and evaluate. The tortuous ratification process of the Maastricht
Treaty in several member states was evidence of growing disquiet – Ireland's 'no to Nice' was, if anything, a belated wake-
up call. The European Union is no longer part of consensus,
non-partisan politics. The end of the era of permissive consensus is to be welcomed.

Robert Dahl has called the democratization of Europe the
'third transformation of democracy'. The first was the birth of
democracy. The second occurred when democracy was trans-
ferred from the theory of Greek city-states to the practice of
modern nation-states. This depiction highlights the magnitude
of the task at hand.[8] In addition, alternatives cannot be evaluated
without an understanding that transnational governance is not
just a consequence of European integration, but also a necessity
in the world today. David Held has argued that 'the problem ...
is that regional and global interconnectedness contests the traditional national resolutions of key questions of democratic theory
and practice. The very process of governance can escape the reach
of the nation-state. National communities by no means exclusively make and determine decisions and policies for themselves,
and governments by no means determine what is appropriate

exclusively for their own citizens.'[9] In the present era of globalization it's quite simple: with or without the EU, mechanisms
are necessary to allow governance beyond the state.

European Law Gains Teeth

The original 1951 ECSC and EEC treaties created law-making
institutions with broad competences. In addition, they provided
for an elaborate system of judicial control. A dedicated court –
the European Court of Justice – was established in Luxembourg, with compulsory jurisdiction, in contrast to most international jurisdictions.[10]

Its two basic roles were to ensure that member states com-
plied with their Community law obligations and to hold the
Community institutions to account. As regards keeping member states in check, the most innovative feature was conferring
prosecutorial power on an independent entity – the European
Commission.[11]

As innovative as this system was, it developed in still further
unanticipated ways. In a series of judgments which predate Ireland's accession, the European Court of Justice interpreted the
provisions of the Treaty as having novel features. The established
principles – worked out in the context of other international
legal instruments, which treat the 'state' as the primary bearer
of rights and responsibilities – were not followed. Rather, European law was held to constitute a 'new legal order', the subjects
of which were not simply states, but also individuals.[12] Thus,
individuals could hold member states to account, and along with
the Commission, would provide 'vigilance' as to compliance
with EU obligations. In addition, European law would take prece-
dence over national law – including national Constitutions.[13]
Later, in addition, an unwritten catalogue of fundamental rights

was read into the Treaties.[14] This was prompted by threats from the German Constitutional Court to override the supremacy of Community law where German constitutional rights were at stake.[15] The European Court of Justice held that fundamental rights formed part of the Community legal order. European law was an autonomous system. This new layer of enforcement was to be carried out in national courts. The ECJ's rhetoric of the autonomy is entirely dependent on national judges co-operation and receptiveness. This has largely been secured, but not without some tensions.

In effect, a dramatic alteration in the constitutional status of the national judges has taken place. National judges were required to hold national governments to account. Such powers are familiar in Ireland in our constitutional set-up, but in other states the effects have been dramatic. For example in the UK, the traditional 'sovereignty of parliament' was set aside in order to ensure the effective enforcement of EU law.[16] Now, seeking a remedy for breach of EU law in the Irish courts is commonplace. In fact, the litigant can claim additional remedies as a matter of Community law.[17]

How is this transformation best captured? What is this new species of law that has been invented?

The most apt language is 'constitutional'. Weiler has commented that community law is 'not merely the Law of the Land but the "Higher Law" of the land. Parallels may ... be found only in the internal constitutional order of federal states.'[18]

The effect of the 'constitutionalization' of the Treaties is that the Community system of judicial control, to a large extent, nationalized Community obligations. With national courts onside, the respect for the rule of law traditionally associated with national obligations is conferred on European obligations. Community provisions are not subject to the whim of national governments. Once a provision is enshrined in the Treaty or enacted in Community legislation, provided certain criteria are fulfilled, individuals may rely on this law before their national courts. Governments ignore Community law at their peril.

One early example concerns the guarantee of equal pay for men and women for equal work.[19] The Treaty article enshrining this guarantee is anomalous in that it displays a social dimension that is not evident in the other original provisions. However, once enshrined in the Treaty, the provision remained dead letter until a series of cases in the 1970s. These were brought by strategic litigants, seeking to ensure that the guarantee would become automatically applicable at the domestic level. The European Court held that the Treaty provision could be invoked directly before national courts, meaning that the failure to introduce European legislation to give effect to the guarantee was no longer decisive.[20] In later years, thousands of Irish women brought similar actions before Irish courts seeking to enforce a later directive on gender equality in social security.[21]

Ireland's Adaptation

Ireland joined what was then the EEC when most of these foundational legal doctrines had been honed. In effect, a normatively superior legal order was being integrated into our own. The Irish Constitution was amended in dramatic fashion to make space for this transformation. Article 29 of the Constitution now permits Ireland's membership of the EU and provides that the Constitution cannot be invoked to invalidate European law or national laws 'necessitated by membership'.[22] In effect, as one Supreme Court judge explained at the time, 'It is as if the people of Ireland had adopted Community law as a second but transcendent Constitution, with the difference that Community law is not to be found in any single document – it is a living growing organism'.[23]

This means that European law applies in Ireland by virtue of the constitutional guarantee in Article 29. In Ireland, as well as elsewhere in Europe, national courts accept European law on their own terms – it applies within the limits of national constitutionality. Thus, possible conflicts arise.

Such conflicts are sometimes cast in absolute terms. My colleague Dr Diarmuid Rossa Phelan has written of the potential for judicial 'Revolt' or legal 'Revolution' inherent in this apparently unstable system.[24] However, to conceive of this system as strictly hierarchical underestimates the degree of interaction between national judges and the European Court of Justice in fashioning this 'new legal order'. Better explanations acknowledge the plurality of legal orders in the EU. Professor Neil Mac-Cormick, legal theorist, Scottish nationalist and MEP, is the leading advocate of this approach. In his vision, 'The most appropriate analysis of the relations of legal systems is pluralistic rather than monistic, interactive rather than hierarchical.'[25]

What are the practical implications of this seemingly abstract theorizing? In practical terms, as already outlined, European law has teeth. De Witte puts it quite simply: 'The individual is at the heart of European law.'[26] More profoundly, the legal subject has changed – we are at once subjects of national and EU law. In effect, the Maastricht inclusion of the status of Citizenship of the Union is declaratory rather than constitutive.

Law-making in the European Union

However, while the features of the legal system are advantageous in terms of holding member states to their Community law bargains, law is also part of the current pathology of the EU. To be a Citizen as rights-bearer only is inadequate. Citizenship properly connotes accountability and political control. What emerges instead is constitutional law without constitutional politics. Thus we must examine not only the advantages that EU law confers, but also the process whereby EU law is made. Part of the problem, as the Nice referendum exposed, is that EU law-making is poorly understood. Let's look at the explanation for this. First, there is inadequate domestic political engagement. While Irish lawyers have proved adept at holding the Irish executive to the bargains it strikes in Brussels, the same cannot be said for domestic parliamentary accountability. Secondly, the variety of EU legislative procedures makes understanding the policy process difficult and calls for sophisticated mechanisms.

Some examples illustrate this diversity. We can contrast at least three scenarios:

First, supranational law-making in relation to the EU's internal market.

Secondly, intergovernmental law-making under the EU provisions on police and judicial co-operation in criminal matters.

Thirdly, an examination of the domestic implementation of EU measures.

Let us turn then to the legislative workings of the EU. The Community method of law-making may be illustrated by a directive adopted in summer 2002 that will prohibit testing of cosmetics on animals.[27] Cosmetics have been regulated at EU level for many years – this was the seventh amendment to the Cosmetics Directive. The influence of the European Parliament was decisive in this outcome. The Commission's original proposal did not ban animal testing, but it revised its proposal after the EP's first reading. Several member state governments opposed the measure, but all that was required was a Qualified Majority Vote among the ministers in the Council. While the deliberations in the Council are still largely held behind closed doors, transparency is ensured, to a degree, by the vigilance of the European Parliament. This method of law-making does of course mean that laws are enacted despite the objections of certain member state governments. However, the role of the European Parliament provides direct European-level democratic input.

An example of intergovernmental law-making serves as a contrast. The Council deliberates such legislation behind closed doors and there is no formal role for the European Parliament. In the immediate aftermath of the terrorist attacks in the USA on 11 September 2001, the Commission put forward a proposal to establish a common EU arrest warrant, ostensibly aimed at 'eliminating legal loopholes in the EU that may help radicals suspected of violence escape justice'. The Council of Ministers adopted the measure in December 2001. The measure is extraordinary in that it is the most ambitious EU measure with implications for criminal law. However, its true distinction is the expedited timeframe in which it was adopted, which precluded adequate debate. Certain national parliaments – in particular in the UK, Sweden and the Netherlands – sought to place a brake on the swift adoption of such a measure, but were unsuccessful. It is only when ample time and information are given in order to allow for adequate deliberation at the national level that the role of national ministers in the Council is legitimate. In such situations, the oft-lauded security of each minister having a veto in the Council proves of little usefulness in terms of legitimacy and accountability of law-making.

The third type of legislative activity to which I want to refer is domestic implementation. Many EU measures require implementation at the national level. Often, this leaves room to adapt

European measures to domestic cultural and legal requirements. In the Irish context, lamentably, this discretion has not been seized or utilized. Most EU measures are implemented by the executive, in other words, effectively by civil servants on behalf of individual government ministers. We have chosen to take the path of least resistance, at some cost to the integrity of our constitutional system. Normally under the Irish Constitution, making law is for the Oireachtas – government may only make detailed implementing measures. However, in the context of implementing EU law, the Irish courts have consistently permitted implementation without parliamentary scrutiny.

The starting point of the constitutional analysis is the Meagher decision of 1994.[28] The Supreme Court's approach was pragmatic, essentially finding that the volume of Community legislation 'necessitated' an expedited form of implementation. It thus justified the mechanism established in the 1970s allowing this executive implementation. This was confirmed in 2001.[29] This modification of the separation of powers has been described as 'one of the most far reaching consequences to date of Ireland's EU membership'.[30] A broad interpretation of 'necessitated' has constitutionally facilitated this transformation, undermining the role of the Oireachtas in EU law-making. Thus the main feature of the EU's democratic deficit, namely the dominance of executive over legislative bodies, has been given a constitutional imprimatur by the Irish judiciary.

What lessons can we learn from these examples?

Media depictions of the EU commonly underestimate the input of the European Parliament. Since the co-decision procedure became widely applicable, the European Parliament has secured strong influence in those predominantly economic areas where this procedure applies.

Secondly, the extent to which unanimity in the Council

guards national prerogative is often overstated. The Arrest Warrant measure illustrates that intergovernmental bargaining
behind closed doors can often lead to smaller member states
being sidelined and national parliaments excluded from decision-making.

Thirdly, each process demands different mechanisms to
ensure legitimacy and accountability. However, many of the
most serious shortcomings are due to failure to engage domes-
tically, rather than any inherent defect at EU level.

Grand Designs

When we examine the current debates, an appreciation of current features and deficits becomes all the more pressing.

The debate on a Constitution for Europe is often portrayed
as implying statehood and a consequent increase in powers for
the EU. However, in legal terms, the EU Treaties are commonly
regarded as 'constitutional'. Few legal commentators find this
contentious, in that constitutional discipline is viewed as inherent in the current system. In addition, the debate outside of Ireland and the UK treats constitutionalism as inherently limitative
of EU competences. In this respect, the loudest advocates of the
proposed more formal Constitution are the German Laender,
anxious to guard the internal vertical separation of powers that
preserves regional diversity within Germany and prevents cen-
tralization. The current constitutional project is thus not a leap
into the unknown, but rather a formalization of the existing constitutional features of the EU.

The substantive issues deliberated at the Convention on the
Future of Europe included

The status of the EU Charter of Fundamental Rights.

The role of national parliaments in EU affairs.

The delimitation of competences between the EU and the
member states.

The simplification of the Treaties.

The current endeavour is risky, in that the proposed Constitutional Treaty may replace some of the more thoughtful features
of the EU and replicate practices in the member states. Early
proposals to create a second chamber of the European Parliament seemed to do just that. If we take just one of these issues,
the debate on the Charter, we can see many of these pitfalls.

The Charter was solemnly declared at Nice in December
2001, having been drafted by a unique convention. Its ostensible
aim was to make the protection of fundamental rights in the EU
more visible. The legal status of the Charter is, as yet, uncer-
tain. It has been included as Part II of the draft Constitutional
Treaty presented by the Convention on the Future of Europe in
June 2003. Despite its non-binding status, the Charter has
already been referred to by several Advocates General of the
European Court of Justice[31] and by the Court of First
Instance,[32] although not by the Court of Justice itself.

The debate on the Charter has been marred by mispercep-
tions as to the protection of fundamental rights in the EU legal
order. Under the current system, the protection of fundamental
human rights in the EU is largely judge-made. The European
Court of Justice draws its inspiration from the 'constitutional
traditions common to the Member States' and the guidelines
supplied by international treaties, in particular the European
Convention on Human Rights, which has been ratified by all
member states (and candidate countries) and incorporated into
domestic law by all except Ireland, although this is imminent.[33]

A significant coterie of EU legal experts thus respond nonchalantly to the Charter, doubting whether it adds anything to the existing legal protections. To them the Charter exercise is one purely of appearances. In this vein, Ulrich Haltern says: 'The Charter has no other use than that associated with consumer aesthetics. The Union wants the Charter to de-stigmatize itself and to neutralize our distrust.'[34]

In contrast, the Irish position seems to be hostile to the Charter for a very different reason. The current Minister for Justice, Equality and Law Reform, speaking in his then capacity as Attorney General, argued that a 'justiciable bill of rights' constitutes one of the 'indiciae of a European state in substance'. For this reason he strongly resisted making the Charter binding.[35] This position seems to both vastly overstate the significance of making visible the existing protections at EU level and also to ignore the entire legal and scholarly body of work devoted to the analysis of the EU's most unique feature – that it has consecrated the rule of law at the supranational level. In other words, it embodies constitutionalism beyond the state. The EU is an entity with broad legislative powers, whose laws impact on citizens directly. It must be legally required to respect fundamental rights and this was acknowledged in the 1970s caselaw of the European Court. To imply such radical transformative effects of drafting an explicit Bill of Rights is grossly misleading.

In addition, there is disquiet in Ireland at the extensive protection for social rights provided in the Charter.[36] This rests on the fallacy that those rights will be directly invoked against the member states, when the Charter is primarily geared at constraining the EU level. It also taps into the current strong domestic legal hostility to the protection of social rights at domestic constitutional level, as exemplified in the Sinnot case.[37]

A more subtle argument later emerged that the Charter was a federalizing endeavour, in that it would lead indirectly to the expansion of the EU's competences. This argument was made by my colleague Dr Gerard Hogan SC,[38] precipitating responses from Eugene Regan BL[39] and me.[40] Dr Hogan's argument has two aspects. First, he suggests that the Charter will come to replace national Constitutions as the benchmark for deciding on the validity of national law, and secondly, he argues that the Charter will give the EU a role in new areas. Both arguments run counter to the text of the Charter and are based on predictions as to likely judicial expansion of the Charter's remit. While not without merit, they do seem to overstate the likelihood of judicial expansion.

This snapshot of the debate on the Charter illustrates the pitfalls of the current period of urgent activity. Unless our starting point is based on a sound understanding of the EU's current features, many misleading arguments may seem plausible. Pragmatic and normative arguments favour governance beyond the state. What is to be feared most of all in current grandiose debates is not that they go 'too far' or not 'far enough' but rather that they are ill-fitting. It is crucial to engage with the debate on the draft Constitutional Treaty. To date discussion and debate in Ireland has been poor. For too long, the Constitution of the EU has been the realm of lawyers and judges. It is time for constitutional law to be matched by constitutional politics.

4. People, Work and Social Change

David Begg

The Nice referendum was very good for democratic politics. For the first time since our accession we had a real debate about the nature of the European project and our relationship to it. For too long Europe was seen through the prism of what was advantageous to us. Our snouts were so deeply in the trough that, as long as the swill kept coming, we didn't need to ask any questions. Apart from those whose business it was to be plugged into Europe the rest of us didn't really concern ourselves with the bigger picture.

The rejection of the first Nice referendum in 2001 was a great shock. It indicated a disconnection from the European project that the élite could not handle. Early reactions were in the nature of asking, 'How could the people be so stupid?' The reality was that no real effort was ever made to promote the broader vision of Europe. For a while we went through a process of various political personalities presenting each other with medals for being 'good Europeans'. Every few years Ireland held the presidency of the Council of Ministers and we were pushed off the road by Garda outriders escorting convoys of darkened Mercedes cars occupied by the Prime Ministers of member states. It was too much like a Latin-American style democracy not to cause resentment. In a country where people expect to be able to meet their politicians face to face and address them by their Christian names, it all seemed too exclusive. It caused a degree of disaffection that came home to roost during the first referendum. We should learn from this experience.

The second referendum campaign was good in that the people, political leaders and representatives of civil society debated the issues in great detail in the media and at public meetings throughout the country. This was real politics and we are entitled, I think, to take a measure of satisfaction from that.

During one of the meetings organized by ICTU one young woman in the audience observed that, in her opinion, Irish people did not really identify with Europe. I instinctively feel that her observation is significant. We don't have the same memories of war that people in other European countries have. Yet many thousands of Irish men fought and died on the European mainland during the two world wars of the last century. The peculiar circumstances of our history have caused us to disown that experience and it has not been without cost in terms of our maturity as a nation.

Last year I visited the battlefields of the Western Front of the First World War. I stood at the site of the Ulster Tower on the Somme battlefield. It's still possible to discern the line of German trenches as they were in July 1916. On the morning of 1 July members of the 36th Ulster Division left their own trenches to assault the German fortification known as the Swaben Redoubt. You wouldn't need to be a military expert to appreciate the impossibility of their task. They had to attack over rising ground against defenders who were well entrenched and had a clear field of fire. Up to fifty thousand fell on that terrible day and they are buried where they fell in front of the German lines. Looking north and south from the Ulster Tower the line of carefully manicured cemeteries marks the Front Line. And so it continued for another two years with men from the 16th and 10th Nationalist Divisions making their sacrifices in further Somme battles and in Flanders too. The vast majority, of course, were workers and trade unionists.

There is a very poignant story told in Padraig Yates' excellent book on the 1913 lockout. It relates how a group of ITGWU men, unable to win reinstatement on the docks, had joined the Dublin Fusiliers *en bloc*. They were part of the regular army that held the line in Flanders while Kitchener's mass volunteer army was training in Britain. On 24 April 1915 they took part in an attack on Saint-Julien, near Ypres. They advanced 'in faultless order' to within a hundred yards of the village, then their line was swept away by machine gunfire. The handful that crawled back gave 'three cheers for Jim Larkin' just as if they were once again outside Liberty Hall.

It may well be that our struggle for independence erased this piece of labour history from our national psyche. No such omission occurred in the case of the German and French workers. They were to the fore in early efforts to establish the European Defence Community. Jean Monnet told American Secretary of State Dulles on 17 December 1954 that 'German Labour considers that European integration is the only way to keep their liberties for the future'.

When the European Defence Community Treaty collapsed the German and French unions continued to support Monnet and ultimately the failed attempt to create a Defence Treaty was superseded by the European Coal and Steel Community. The unions viewed this initiative as breaking the power of the coal and steel barons, whom they saw as being at least partially responsible for the war.

By 1955 Monnet was working on establishing the Action Committee, which led to the formation of the Common Market. According to his biographer, François Duchêne, a note in his diary for 4 January 1955, envisaged a committee of leading individuals from political parties and trade unions, with first priority on the 'free trade unions of the West'. For Monnet, an action committee's resolutions had to commit member political parties and labour unions and so have institutional force. He drew the line at European movements and employers' federations. He thought employers incapable of distinguishing the general interest from their own. He felt that the labour unions had a better sense of it because they represented broad masses.

The trade unions remained loyal supporters of Monnet even to the point of bankrolling his campaigning work up until his death. The European Trade Union Confederation remains deeply integrationist in outlook to this day.

But if the Europeans were strong supporters of the Common Market their Irish counterparts were more sceptical. When the 465 delegates to the annual delegate conference of the Irish Congress of Trade Unions gathered in Limerick in July 1971, one of the most contentious and important subjects for debate was the question of Ireland's proposed membership of the European Economic Community (EEC). Six motions on this topic had been placed on the agenda for debate. Some of them advocated outright opposition to EEC membership while others expressed qualified support. A composite, comprehensive motion was debated and adopted by the conference.

This motion expressed serious concern with 'all aspects of the proposed accession of Ireland to the EEC'. It was critical of the government's failure to adequately survey and quantify the effects of membership on employment and workers' living standards and its failure to get the EEC to recognize the special industrial and regional development needs of Ireland. It expressed concern about loss of effective control of political and economic policy and possible involvement in military commitments, and it concluded by stating that the conference could not express any support for the proposed entry of Ireland given the inadequacy of the information available. Adoption of this motion would not therefore amount to a clear-cut decision to oppose EEC membership *per se*, but would be an interim decision to withhold support for EEC membership at that stage because of the dearth of information and the perceived weakness of the Irish negotiating position.

Subsequently a campaign committee was established that was chaired by Senator Fintan Kennedy (President, ITGWU and Treasurer of Congress). The campaign committee concentrated on the publication and dissemination of an eight-page broadsheet paper entitled 'Economic Freedom'. It comprehensively analysed the economic implications of EEC membership. It presented detailed data on production and employment in individual sectors. It vigorously promoted the view that there were viable alternatives to EEC membership and focused on the cost of living increases that EEC membership would inevitably bring with it. The Irish people, in their wisdom, rejected this advice and voted in favour of membership by a substantial majority.

The involvement of a substantial number of senior trade union leaders in European-level activities had a major impact on their thinking and attitudes towards the EEC. Congress had also moved to affiliate to the European Trade Union Confederation (ETUC) and this was formally accepted in March 1974. This broadened significantly the perspective of Irish trade unions beyond the traditional close links with the British trade union movement which, for historical and practical reasons, had a very strong influence on Irish trade unions.

The equal pay debate that erupted in 1974 brought the Irish trade union movement face to face with the procedures and institutions of the EEC in an effort to secure the basic right to equal pay for equal work for women. This would be the first test of the practical value to Irish workers of the lofty principles of the Treaty of Rome.

The Anti-Discrimination (Pay) bill was published in February 1974 to transpose the European Directive into Irish law. Even though Congress had serious reservations about many of the provisions of the bill that did not go as far as similar legislation in Northern Ireland, the Act was passed in July 1974 and provided for full implementation of equal pay by 31 December 1975 in accordance with the European deadline. However, on 17 December 1975 the Taoiseach, Liam Cosgrave, announced in the Dáil that the government had decided that amendments were necessary to the Act before it came into force. Congress immediately notified the government that in the event of the non-implementation of the Act, it would lodge a formal complaint to the European Commission. The government persisted in deferring implementation and sought derogation from the Commission. Congress forwarded a comprehensive submission to the European Commission in February 1976 opposing the application by the government for derogation.

On 5 May 1976 the Minister for Labour informed the Dáil that the government had received a formal communication from the European Commission rejecting the government's application for a derogation from the provision of the Equal Pay Directive and that in consequence, the government would not now be proceeding with the proposed amending legislation.

This represented an outright victory for the trade unions

with the European Commission as a strong ally. It was a very public engagement and pitched the trade unions and the European Commission together against the Irish government. It guaranteed the timely enactment of one of the most significant pieces of employment legislation. It transformed the Irish workplace for women and shattered the stereotype of the EEC as being only the voice of big business and capital.

Prior to our involvement with Europe, social policy in Ireland was strongly influenced by Catholic social teaching. It was generally understood to mean policy on social welfare, health, education and housing. Ireland never achieved a classical welfare state. What we have has been described as 'a mixed economy of welfare' containing a strong component delivered through the voluntary sector. This accounts for approximately Ir£480 million directly with a further Ir£120 million coming from the European Union.

European Union social policy has been hugely influential in the progressive development of Irish social policy, particularly in the field of equality. The Equal Pay Directive gave impetus to the implementation of Irish legislation. In more recent progressive decisions, such as the incremental progression and seniority for job sharers/part-time workers, we have achieved progress that would not otherwise have been made.

Trade unions have been able to successfully petition the European Court of Justice on a number of occasions and the independence and accessibility of that institution is highly respected.

Other major social policy developments have also impacted on Ireland. In December 1989 we adopted the Community Charter of Fundamental Social Rights of Workers (the Social Chapter). The Maastricht Treaty introduced a detailed consultative procedure between the Commission, employers and unions on social policy, enabling the social partners to conclude agreements at

European level. These agreements have led to the introduction in Ireland of parental leave and important rights for part-time workers and those on fixed-term contracts. In his paper 'Recasting the European Social Model' Peter Cassells has described the context in which the Delors vision for social Europe led to the establishment of the partnership process in Ireland. It is important to reiterate that our experience in Ireland remains located within a vision of social solidarity between the peoples of Europe that has yet to find its proper balance with the economic agenda of Europe.

The publication in 1994 of the White Paper on Growth, Competitiveness and Employment in Ireland broadened the debate on economic policy beyond the narrow confines of monetary issues, deregulation and cutting wage costs. It examined the interlinked issues of investing for the future, competitiveness, innovation and positive flexibility. This paper, while endorsing the European model of development, recognized that it required renewal and adjustment and that European countries must compete with the best in the world through high productivity, high levels of quality and high standards. The Amsterdam Treaty empowered the EU to take action to combat discrimination based on gender, race, religion, age, disability and sexual orientation, and provided for co-operation between the member states to fight social exclusion.

Apart from its impact on the evolution of social policy, membership of the European Union was good for Irish workers in economic terms too, although the benefits did take nearly twenty years to materialize. Until around 1994, evaluations of the Irish economy generally concluded that Ireland had failed. In 1913 Irish real product per capita was twice the Japanese level; but by 1985 it was half the Japanese level. There was no obvious excuse for this slippage. At independence Ireland had a literate population, good infrastructure, substantial foreign assets and a functioning bureaucracy. It was close to some of the world's biggest markets. It had substantial natural resources of soil and sea, if not iron and coal. The destruction of war bypassed the country. Historian Joe Lee blames Ireland's poor economic performance on an unimaginative civil service and a corrosive ethic of 'begrudgery', and argues that Anglophone Ireland, because it did not need to make an effort to learn other languages and cultures, followed British ways too closely.

What a difference five years make. After half a decade of exceptionally rapid growth, Irish GDP is now well above the EU mean, and indicators of living standards – car registrations, consumption per capita, life expectancy – are catching up fast too. Historians and economists are quickly adjusting their assessment of Irish performance, acknowledging the newfound affluence and regretting it did not arrive sooner.

It is hard to pinpoint specific events that caused the acceleration of Irish economic growth in the mid-1990s. The investment rate did not suddenly rise; the EU single market did not drop manna-like from heaven; EU subventions remained steady or even fell, as did domestic subsidies to industry. There were no dramatic changes in taxes or educational levels or the age of the labour force.

A more plausible view is that the economic planets all came into alignment at the same time. The key elements would seem to be: a booming US economy providing firms there with the profits to invest abroad; a 10 per cent tax on manufacturing profits to attract them to Ireland; the lure of a large pool of a well-educated and hard-working labour force; the creation of a Single European Market that could be served efficiently from English-speaking Ireland and the stability created by successive social partnership agreements.

EU economic influence is not necessarily benign in all respects. In the course of the Nice referendum campaign many of those advocating a 'No' vote asserted that Article 133 of the Treaty would give rise to extensive liberalization and eventually privatization of public services. They were correct in believing that this is an integral part of EU economic policy as it stands but wrong in suggesting that it is a constituent part of the Nice Treaty.

The threat to the public sector comes from what is known as the 'Cardiff Process'. This was initiated during the British Presidency in 1998 and according to Professor Roy Green of UCG was designed to ensure that structural reform and competition policy gained a foothold in the European economic agenda. It is now part of a much broader process of developing the knowledge-based economy as outlined at the Lisbon and Stockholm summits. The key elements of product and capital market liberalization remain central to the process. The evidence suggests that the Council of Finance Ministers (ECOFIN) is and will continue to be the dominant influence in policy formation, delivery and, ultimately, enforcement. This influence has a narrow, even ideological basis in neoliberal microeconomic orthodoxy and assumes that perfectly competitive markets will by definition always generate optimal efficiency and consumer welfare and that, correspondingly, 'imperfections' and impediments to freely operating markets will result in less than optimal outcomes and must therefore be eliminated through structural reform. So far, impediments in product, services and capital markets to be identified include 'public monopoly' ownership structures, barriers to market entry and national systems of regulation and industrial support. Measures to address these impediments have involved privatization, deregulation and competition policy.

The future of the Cardiff Process raises two questions. First, will this narrow vision of structural reform become the guiding theme of efforts to build the 'most competitive knowledge-based economy in the world'? Will governments and the social partners be prepared to think more creatively about the next stages of development of the European social model, which may require well-targeted instruments of intervention to build dynamic national and regional systems of innovation with scope for involvement by workers and their unions? Significantly, the National Competitiveness Council has called upon the government to draw up a national policy on regulatory reform and the institutional framework through which reform would be pursued, having 'regard to wider social objectives' (NCC 2000).

The second question is whether the broadening of the Cardiff Process at the Lisbon and Stockholm summits will increase the likelihood that reform of product and capital markets will 'spill over' to the labour market, and possibly incorporate reform in this area into the overall agenda. The problem here is that textbook impediments to the operation of labour markets include minimum wage regulation, welfare benefits and trade union organization, all of which are said to have the effect of keeping wages above their market clearing levels, hence creating an excess supply of labour. It is only one short step from this argument to suggest that the solution to unemployment lies in removing these impediments, despite the role they might play in improving the productivity of firms, protecting individual employees, ensuring fair pay in an increasingly fragmented labour market and contributing to social stability.

It can be argued that the Irish labour market has so far been relatively insulated from the worst aspects of structural reform. However, the union movement is aware of the dangers, and we are not confident that these can be forestalled without stronger EU regulation. The most serious danger arises from the introduction of competition into areas of public sector monopoly, such as rail and bus transport, which may provide opportunities for quality improvement but often leads instead to low-wage competition and under-investment in a 'race to the bottom'. Further, the privatization of state enterprises will generally require a new style of management and industrial relations that maximizes shareholder value, possibly at the expense of job security and rights of union representation. This is particularly the case if the enterprise is broken up to focus on its 'core business', which also implies abandoning community service obligations. Finally, the creation of a competitive business environment also reinforces the overall shift to more flexible labour markets, including ever-growing gaps between high skill, secure workers and those in low paid, marginalized and precarious employment.

The Cardiff Process may well enable EU governments and the social partners to reflect upon what is advantageous and distinctive about the European social model, by contrast with the deregulated markets, economic inequalities and minimal infrastructure of US capitalism. It will help define the issue of what kind of policy framework is required for balanced and sustainable success as a knowledge-based economy.

I have serious reservations about the model of conservative capitalism radiating out from the United States to the rest of the world. The growing consensus among economists is that the current American economic downturn will be short-lived and the dynamic US economy will leap back into life courtesy of cheap oil and very low interest rates. The US will do it on its own. But the financial system has taken a major hit, and US consumers and business alike are chronically indebted. The US will be forced towards an adjustment of its ambitions and living standards; it will resist, and things will get ugly. The US has already unilaterally imposed swinging tariffs to save its beleaguered but uncompetitive steel industry, in abuse of world trade rules. The EU is cautioned against any retaliation, even if within the WTO's rules. Now it's one rule for the US, another for the rest of the world.

American capitalism is a great deal weaker than it likes to claim and American society is seriously disfigured by the results of the way the economy is run. The US has been able to escape – so far – the social consequences of its economic structures, both because of the commonly accepted myth of its exceptional social mobility and also because of its profound cultural attachment to particular ideas of liberty that excuse social suffering. No such avenue is open to the Europeans. European society cannot willingly turn a blind eye to the corruption and deformation of its democracy by the forces of rapacious inequality.

A close examination of the operation of the two systems' labour markets shows that, for all their vaunted flexibility, the American labour market works less well and European markets better than either is supposed to. American workers' chances of moving out of low-paid jobs are smaller; turnover rates are not especially high; and unemployment in low-skilled jobs relative to high-skilled jobs is higher than in 'regulated' Europe.

As for the structure of the financial system, the US is already having cause to ponder whether the dot-com and telecoms bubbles were worth the financial deregulation that spawned them. Rarely has the world witnessed such capricious and vacuous venality dressed up as 'enterprise'; rarely have so many been gulled by such duplicity.

European civilization is underpinned by values that Europe's leaders could not give up even if they wanted to. Their roots lie deep and define what it means to be a European. American conservatism, having wrought contemptible damage on its own society, cannot be allowed to repeat the carnage in Europe. The

European belief that the wealthy and propertied have reciprocal obligations to the society of which they are part and which cannot be discharged by charity alone goes back to early Christendom – as does the associated notion that a settled people must form a social contract to entrench their association. This in turn demands a public realm that permits the articulation and expression of what we hold in common. It is these propositions that, when turned into structures and policies, produce the high-quality social outcomes that distinguish Europe from the US. The conservative American attack on these values, poorly challenged by liberals in the US, must be better resisted in Europe. We must turn back the tide in the name of the good society and common humanity.

The former French Prime Minister, Lionel Jospin, in a speech to the Foreign Press Association in May 2001, described a 'Plan for Society' with which I very much agree.

> Until a recent period, the essential efforts of Europe were concentrated on the putting in place of an economic and monetary union from which we have reaped real benefits ...
>
> Europe is much more than just a market ... There is an 'art of living' that belongs to Europeans ... battling against inequalities and discriminations ... thinking ... industrial relations ... teaching ... caring ... using time well.
>
> This model must henceforth be written into Treaties and must come alive in our policies. Remember that Europe is a civilization, that is to say a territory, a shared history, a unified economy, a humane society and a cultural diversity that draws together a culture.

5. Irish Politics and European Politics

Brigid Laffan

In January 1972 Taoiseach Jack Lynch and his Foreign Minister, Dr Patrick Hillery, left Dublin airport for Brussels to sign Ireland's Treaty of Accession to what was then called the European Community, now known as the European Union. Just over fifty years after the signing of the Anglo-Irish Treaty, a treaty that gave the people of 26 of the 32 counties on the island of Ireland the right to establish a state separate from the United Kingdom, an Irish government negotiated membership of a Community that involved a sharing or pooling of sovereignty with other states within the framework of treaties and collective institutions.

The Taoiseach and his party were seen off at Dublin airport by the then President, Eamon de Valera. The photograph capturing the departing Taoiseach and the ageing President was hugely symbolic. This tableau captured the ties but also the tensions between the Ireland of 1972 and the Ireland of 1916. Jack Lynch's departure to sign the Rome Treaties represented the end of the Ireland that de Valera would have wished for and experienced. Right up to the mid-1950s de Valera's idea or ideal of Ireland was that of a rural and preferably Gaelic-speaking society committed to spiritual rather than material values. The Ireland of the twenties, thirties, forties and fifties was an Ireland fearful of the consequences of economic modernization, urbanization and growth.

By the end of the fifties Ken Whitaker, the Secretary of the Department of Finance, and the new Fianna Fáil Taoiseach, Seán Lemass, were determined to liberalize and internationalize the Irish economy and, as a consequence, Irish society. In 1958 Ken Whitaker was responsible for penning the *Little Grey Book on Economic Development*, a report that set out the strategy Ireland would adopt in search of economic modernization. The report strongly advocated the abandonment of protectionism and an acceptance of free trade. The desire for membership of the EU was a logical consequence of the change in economic strategy. Membership of the EU would serve the dual objective of reducing Ireland's dependence on Britain and providing a large liberalizing market for Irish products. Ireland made its first application for membership on 31 July 1961 and it took a further twelve years to bring this goal to fruition. Seán Lemass, an old man in a hurry, proved capable of mediating between Ireland's past and its future. It was his successor Jack Lynch who signed the Treaty of Accession and secured victory in the referendum that endorsed Ireland's membership of the Union. Eighty-three per cent of those who voted supported Ireland's membership of the EU. Membership was thus the 'settled will' of the Irish people. The size of the 'yes' vote and the absence of divisions on Europe within the main political parties ensured that Ireland's adjustment to membership would be much smoother than either of the other two states – the United Kingdom and Denmark – that joined on the same date.

Joining the European Union was different to joining a traditional international organization in a number of important respects. First, the European Court of Justice (ECJ) has transformed the treaties of the EU into a constitutional framework that limits the legal sovereignty of each member state. We now operate within a dual constitutional framework – the national and the European. Second, the decision-making processes of the EU are designed to foster collective agreements by the sharing or pooling of member state sovereignty. The sharing of sovereignty ultimately transforms its exercise. Third, membership of the Union implies a commitment to active participation in the institutions of the Union, the Commission, the Council of Ministers, and the European Parliament. Fourth, membership of the EU implies a commitment to the EU as it evolves and not just as it is when a state first joins the club.

These four characteristics of the Union when taken together imply that the member states submit to a 'shared destiny'. After 1973 the Irish political system was locked into a shared arena above the level of the state. The old distinction between foreign policy and domestic politics, between the state and its external environment broke down. A new kind of politics, EU politics, became part and parcel of how we are governed.

In the pre-accession period, political attention was focused on negotiating the Accession Treaty and on the referendum. Very little political thought was given to living with the EU system once we were in. The impact of membership on Irish politics was most keenly felt in the government and civil service in the initial phase of membership. Government ministers began to go to Brussels to attend Council meetings and Irish civil servants took up their places in Council and Commission working parties. Dr Patrick Hillery, Ireland's first Commissioner, took up office in Brussels. The Irish mission in Brussels became the Irish Permanent Representation, a microcosm of the Irish administration.

Unlike traditional embassies, the Representation draws its staff from across the Irish system. Most government departments have their people in Brussels.

Early-morning flights to Brussels became part of the day-to-day pattern of ministers and their officials. They had just two years to learn the rules of the Brussels system before Ireland had to take responsibility for the Presidency of the Council in 1975 and the first European Council in December of that year. The public service found itself short of the staff needed to manage the administrative demands of membership. The key departments, particularly Foreign Affairs, got additional staff to cope. Notwithstanding the additional demands on ministers and civil servants, there was an openness to participation in the EU throughout the Irish public administration. Dr Garret FitzGerald, the then Foreign Minister, in speeches at the time spoke of the psychological benefits of membership in the following terms:

> For those of us who have in one way or another the task of representing Ireland's in the Community, there is, of course, the exhilaration of finding ourselves, at last, participating fully and on an equal footing with our partners in efforts to organise, run and develop the Economic Community itself.

Thirty years of membership may well have dimmed that early exhilaration. Ireland's apprenticeship in the Union ended with the successful Presidency of the Council in 1975. Since then, Ireland has run five additional successful Presidencies and will take over the mantle again in the first half of 2004.

Although the tentacles of the EU reached into the Irish governmental system and Irish ministers and civil servants actively engaged in Brussels, the impact of the Union on the wider political system was muted. A broad political consensus on Ireland's involvement in the Union meant that there was little contention about European issues in the media and in the Oireachtas. The

Joint Committee on Secondary Legislation was established in
1974 by the Oireachtas to oversee the use of secondary legislation in the implementation of EC law. A lack of resources, weak
knowledge of Community law, and the absence of a tradition of
committees in Irish parliamentary culture made it difficult for
the new Joint Committee to develop a strong system of parliamentary scrutiny. Senator Mary Robinson, almost on her own,
attempted to keep an eye on what Irish governments were agree-
ing to in Brussels. The Joint Committee was, however, an important experiment in the use of parliamentary committees and fed
into the later expansion of such parliamentary committees.

The pervasive localism of Irish politics and multi-member
constituencies meant that relatively few Irish parliamentarians
developed an interest in and grasp of EU policies and politics.
Deep knowledge of Europe was the preserve of those who were
serving or had served as ministers in the Council. This meant
that Irish government ministers and their civil servants did not
face the challenge of participating in EU policy-making in a hostile political or parliamentary environment. They did not have
to control, disguise or attempt to contain the impact of EU policy at national level. Rather, successive governments and the
senior civil service were largely free to chart Ireland's course in
the EU. Consensus at home made it much easier to engage in the
politics of the Union.

Irish political parties could not ignore the EU because they
had to send MEPs to the parliament from the outset. Until direct
elections in 1979, Ireland's MEPs were drawn from the Dáil and
served under a 'dual mandate'. The European Parliament works
on the basis of political groupings rather than national delega-
tions. The three main parties – Fianna Fáil, Fine Gael, and
Labour – had to become members of broader European groups.
Labour joined the European Socialists, Fine Gael the Christian

Democrats and Fianna Fáil were left in a 'marriage of convenience' with the French Gaullists. Paradoxically, the largest Irish political party found itself in a relatively peripheral parliamentary grouping in the Union. From 1979 onwards, direct elections to the European Parliament became part of the electoral calendar in Ireland and these elections provided an additional source of electoral competition. The three parties were later joined by the Greens and Pat Cox, a member of the Liberal grouping. Pat Cox is undoubtedly the most successful Irish MEP. He first became leader of the Liberal grouping and in 2002, President of the European Parliament. In this role, he has political responsibility for a European institution and is engaged in European politics at the highest level.

The shift of decision-making to Brussels in a number of important policy areas brought Irish-interest organizations into the Brussels arena. The employers' organizations and farming groups established their own offices in Brussels and became part of Europe-wide confederations. The trade unions, although they did not have the financial resources for a full Brussels office, joined the European Trade Union Confederation (ETUC). Environmental groups, anti-poverty networks, women's groups, consumer interests, chambers of commerce and many others in Brussels later joined the social partners. There is a very active involvement of Irish voluntary groups in Commission advisory committees and networks. Domestic interest groups are no longer confined to domestic politics. They have followed legislative power to Brussels. In lobbying parlance, they need to 'shoot where the ducks are' and some of the ducks are now in Brussels. All have become players in the multi-levelled politics of the Union. All seek to influence not just the Irish government but decision-making processes in the EU.

The impact of the EU on government and politics was not

restricted to the projection of Irish interests in Brussels but became part of domestic change in a number of areas. The first is social partnership. Ireland found itself in dire economic straits in the 1980s. Without radical change, the opportunities offered by the EU's internal market would have been lost. Gradually there was recognition by government and the key representatives of the two sides of industry of the need for change.

Irish efforts to manage the internationalization of the economy evolved through a form of neo-corporatism known as social partnership. This began in 1987 with the Programme for National Recovery (1987–90) and was followed by a number of subsequent programmes. The programmes involved agreement between employers, trade unions, farming interests and the government on wage levels in the public and private sectors and on a wide range of economic and social policies. The content of all programmes was negotiated in the context of EU developments and the need to ensure that Ireland adjusted to the demands of economic integration. The ability to move from adversarial relations to partnership was in some measure due to EU engagement. The employers and trade unionists learnt of the value of partnership when exposed to continental European practices, and not just the British adversarial system. The partnership approach together with an expansion of EU spending programmes in Ireland and a significant increase in US investment produced the much-needed recovery from the disastrous early and mid-1980s. From 1992 onwards, Ireland consistently outperformed its EU partners in terms of economic growth, employment creation and the growth of exports.

Ireland joined the EU as a highly centralized state with weak central government and a non-existent regional tier. The EU has had a limited impact on territorial politics in Ireland. The structural funds are the main European instrument to assist the development of the peripheral regions of Europe and, for the purposes of the structural funds, Ireland was designated as one region until 2000 when the country was divided into two regions. The Commission was and continues to be an advocate of partnership as a principle of government. It encourages the involvement of regions and local government in decision-making on how EU monies are spent. In response to Commission pressure, the highly centralized nature of Irish public policy making was loosened somewhat and regional structures were established. The original regional structures, established in 1988, were largely an administrative expedient that added a weak regional layer to the implementation of the Community Support Framework (CSF) and thereby satisfied the Commission. However, the resurgence of community groups in Ireland and the need to tackle economic black spots led to a renewed focus on the local in the second national plan. Community initiatives such as LEADER, area-based partnerships, and the County Enterprise Boards all reinforced the territorial dimension of development but were not in themselves capable of giving Ireland effective local and regional government. The organization of sub-national government in Ireland has been the subject of more consultative papers than any other aspect of government but it is also one that has never been tackled with political energy and determination.

The management of the structural funds, which was contained within the narrow confines of central government and the large state sponsored bodies, has evolved to include diffuse interests including local authorities, community groups, environmental groups, and the social partners, all in search of a slice of the Brussels pie. EU monies created a new kind of politics that encouraged people to look both below and beyond the state. Access to EU monies gave community groups additional authority and leverage *vis-à-vis* central government. The availability of Brussels money encouraged the Irish public service to engage in experimentation and micro-social interventions. On the other hand, the availability of EU largesse also reinforced clientalism, a central feature of the political culture.

The secular increase in regulations emanating from the EU had a major impact on the shaping of regulations in many areas of public policy, such as state aids, company law, telecoms, environmental law and health and safety. In response to EU developments and the need to modernize the regulatory framework in Ireland, there was considerable institution-building with, for example, the establishment of the Employment Equality Agency, the Health and Safety Authority and the Environmental Protection Agency. These agencies would have evolved with or without EU membership as Ireland was transformed from an agricultural economy to an industrial and service-oriented one, but EU membership provided the regulatory context for these agencies and shaped their development. All of these agencies have extensive contact with the Commission and their counterparts in other member states. The growth of these agencies highlights the importance of regulation in contemporary politics. This style of politics involves the delegation of authority to regulatory agencies and is heavily reliant on expertise and technical knowledge.

The Irish electorate has had to endorse the constitutional development of the European Union in a number of referenda since the membership vote in 1972, when 83 per cent of the electorate voted in favour. Since the Single European Act was negotiated in the mid-1980s, there have been five further referenda – on the Single Act (1987), the Treaty on European Union (1992), the Treaty of Amsterdam (1998) and on the Treaty of Nice (2001 and 2002). The size of the 'yes' vote declined from the high of 83 per cent in 1972 to 62 per cent in 1998 for the

Treaty of Amsterdam. Acceptance of Ireland's involvement in European integration appeared well-rooted in the Irish body politic and in surveys over many years. Well over 80 per cent of respondents believe that membership has been good to Ireland. In Eurobarometer 48 (autumn 1997), 88 per cent of Irish respondents felt that Ireland had benefited from membership. This was a higher proportion than for other member states. A high level of knowledge about EU affairs, however, did not accompany support for Ireland's membership of the Union. Ireland ranked just above the Union average in knowledge of European affairs. Richard Sinnott found in 1995 that 59 per cent of Irish respondents to Eurobarometer surveys displayed low or very low knowledge of the EU.

Ireland was the only member state that had to submit the Nice Treaty to a popular referendum for constitutional reasons. On 7 June 2001, the Irish electorate voted 'no' to the Nice Treaty by 53.87 per cent to 46.13 per cent, in an extremely low turnout of just 34.8 per cent. People were unwilling to vote for a treaty that they did not have a grasp of in any meaningful sense. They were unwilling to vote 'yes' on the basis of the government saying that the Treaty was a necessary and good thing. The outcome of the referendum was a major reversal for the government that had negotiated the Treaty, for the main opposition parties that had advocated a 'yes' vote and for the peak groups in civil society, notably the main business associations, farming organizations and the trade union congress. There is no doubt that the 'no' side not only won the referendum, but also conducted the most effective campaign. In contrast, the 'yes' campaign lacked vision and conviction. It clearly failed in its responsibility to mobilize the 'yes' vote that had been available in previous referenda.

The performance of the government was particularly lacklustre as it appeared to take the outcome and the electorate for granted. The Taoiseach and the Minister for Foreign Affairs engaged in public debate but other government ministers were notable by their low visibility. The main opposition parties, although they supported the treaty, also failed to campaign. The 'yes' supporters were successfully portrayed as part of a tired establishment out of touch with the Irish public.

The rejection of the Treaty had a major impact on Ireland's relations with the EU, the member states and the candidate countries in east central Europe. Ireland's previous status as a reasonably community-minded member state was openly questioned by other member states. A relatively stable institutional and political relationship was cut loose of its moorings. At home, a debate opened up about the future direction of the EU and Ireland's position in that Union. The government was faced with the challenge of regaining the support of the Irish public on Europe and managing its relations with its partners in the Union and future partners in central Europe. From the outset, the government wanted to create the conditions that would allow it to go back to the Irish people again. The government was very conscious of the damage to Ireland's presence in the Union, if this small state, a state that did so well from membership of the EU was seen to delay or disrupt enlargement. Notwithstanding the democratic dilemma involved, the Irish electorate was asked to revisit the Nice Treaty and give its final answer.

The government established a national Forum on Europe in the immediate aftermath of the first referendum in order to tease out the electorate's knowledge about the European Union and Ireland's engagement with it. The Forum consisted of representatives of the political parties with representation in the two houses of parliament and an observer pillar of interested civil society groups. The Forum met in public in Dublin and throughout the country. It provided a formal channel for a debate on all aspects of the EU and the Nice Treaty. The debate tended to be highly stylized with a restatement of the basic positions (pro or anti) from the political parties. However, it brought into the debate that was taking place in Ireland prime ministers, ministers, officials, MEPs, national parliamentarians and academics from the other member states and the candidate countries. The active engagement of fellow Europeans in an internal Irish debate was legitimized and welcomed. Fellow Europeans did not come to preach but to engage in a lively debate with the Irish political class and the wider society about the future of the Union. In the Forum, it was impossible to see where Irish politics ended and European politics began.

The referendum was scheduled for autumn 2002 following the successful re-election of the Irish government in May. The second referendum was very different to the first both in its conduct and outcome. The outcome was a decisive 'yes' from 63 per cent of the turnout. The turnout of 49 per cent was significantly up from the previous referendum and the vast majority of the additional voters voted 'yes'. The 'no' vote increased by some 400 votes whereas the 'yes' vote increased by just under half a million. The second campaign was characterized by far higher mobilization on the part of the government parties, the pro-EU opposition parties and civil-society groups.

A Convention on the Future of Europe was convened in Brussels in March 2002 to explore the constitutional and institutional framework of an enlarged Europe of twenty-five or more states. Its remit is very broad but one of its main themes is how the EU can be brought closer to Europe's citizens. The Irish experience of Nice has important lessons both for the EU and wider Europe and we should ensure that these lessons are communicated to European institutions and the other member states.

Four lessons stand out. The first lesson is that the legitimacy of the European Union cannot be secured only on the basis of benefits. In Ireland there is a high level of support for membership of the EU and a high level of awareness of the benefits of the EU but this on its own could not secure the ratification of Nice I. The electorate would not be taken for granted. Governments and EU institutions must begin to communicate politically about Europe.

Second, much of the debate on the democratic deficit misses the crucial insight that you cannot have democracy without politics. All of the discourse on European citizenship and a European identity fails to acknowledge that political identity will only develop if there are opportunities to participate in politics. Without politics there cannot be a European public space. Creating a participatory democracy in Europe is an experiment and the only way of proceeding is to create political opportunities for participation.

The third lesson is that national electorates can deal with issues that are of European and not just national importance. It became apparent during the campaign that the electorate understood that its decision was not just an Irish decision but one that had implications for Ireland's partners – both present and future – in the EU and in central Europe. The electorate did not use the opportunity to punish the incumbent government. It was able to distinguish between domestic and European politics.

Fourth, the experience of Nice I and II suggests that an electorate will grapple with European issues, however technical, if they feel they are important enough. During the second Nice referendum many voters worked hard to improve their appreciation of the issues and read the information that was pouring through their doors, and listened to the debates on radio and television. Quite simply, Europe and Ireland's engagement with it cannot come alive without politicization and contestation.

6. The Economics of EU Membership

Garret FitzGerald

In 1957 the European Community was created by the Treaty of Rome, which contained a commitment to establish by the year 1970 a common agricultural policy with a single price level. Precisely what that price level would be was not clear, but it was obvious that it would be fixed somewhere between the highest and lowest price levels of the existing Community. And even the lowest farm price level in any of the six founding member states was well above that available to Irish farmers in the only market that was then open to them – neighbouring Britain.

For over a century Britain had been pursuing a 'cheap food' policy, allowing overseas farm products freely into its market, so as to keep down food prices – and thus wages. In that way the British sought to preserve their competitive advantage in respect of their manufactured exports in the face of growing competition from other industrializing countries. This British policy had held back the Irish economy, which, outside the industrialized Belfast region, was predominantly agricultural. In a Europe where all other states protected their agricultural sectors, political independence brought no relief to Irish agriculture, for which the depressed British market remained the only available outlet.

In principle, at least, the new European Community was open to other European states, and for a largely agricultural country like Ireland, membership at some time in the future could be very attractive: it must be recalled that at the time of which I speak – the late 1950s – three out of every eight Irish workers were still engaged in farming.

At that time there were proposals, which fizzled only out at the end of 1958, to create a free trade area that would encompass both the new Community and the rest of Western Europe. Britain was to be a member. And Ireland, so closely linked by trade to Britain, could not afford to be left out of such a project. We were therefore seeking to participate, on a basis that would involve phasing out industrial protection over a very long twenty-year period. But it was not clear that we would in fact be given such a long transition period within which to free our industrial trade.

Thus, one way or the other, it was clear in 1958 that the small Irish manufacturing sector, notably inefficient and high-cost behind its very high protective barriers, was going to have to face a major shake-up. And, if it could be successfully prepared for free trade within a reasonable period, we might at some stage be able to join the European Community itself, to the huge advantage of our depressed agricultural sector.

At that time I was Research and Schedules Manager of Aer Lingus. Although very happy in my job, I had started to think that it might be time to move on to a broader involvement in the economic sphere, and perhaps also eventually in politics. And it seemed to me that there was clearly a challenge for me there. So, securing a one-year research position at Trinity College, I left Aer Lingus and embarked upon a project that would require me to contact several hundred industrial firms and to visit several score of them. This was in the hope that these contacts might eventually enable me to get involved in the process of preparing Irish industry for free trade. As almost none of our qualified academic economists were interested in our small industrial sector, this was not as long a shot as one might think.

Before my year in Trinity was up, Seán Lemass had been elected Taoiseach, thus giving a new impetus to the recently adopted process of reversing the inward-looking protectionism of the past. For he soon made it clear that we must prepare at least to become an associate of the new Community, even if it was not clear that we could yet aspire to full membership.

By this time I had become a member of the UCD Political Economy Department and with a UCD colleague I soon found myself engaged in a pilot study of one protected industrial sector. In our report on that sector we recommended that, in order to prepare for free trade within the European Community, the government and the Federation of Irish Industries – the IBEC of that time – should join together to review the whole of the Irish manufacturing sector.

In mid-1961 this recommendation was accepted, at about the same time as Seán Lemass, to the surprise of most people, announced that, in parallel with Britain, we were going to apply for full membership of the Community, rather than just association – which would not have benefited agriculture. Thereafter, for a number of years, as part-time economic consultant to the Federation of Irish Industries, I was actively engaged in this industrial review process.

What needs to be stressed today is that all this action in the industrial sector was seen primarily as a defensive measure – one designed to minimize losses in a weak industrial sector in order that we might secure what were seen as great economic benefits for our farm sector.

It is true that we were also starting to seek out multinational firms that might help to fill gaps left by any native industries that failed to adapt to free trade conditions. Nevertheless, it was in agriculture rather than in industry that most people then believed our future to lie. For agriculture would become prosperous as a result of Ireland, together with Britain, joining the European Community, because within that Community Britain would no longer be free to pursue its 'cheap food' policy. With the emergence in due course of a Common Agricultural Policy and a single European price system, Irish farmers would for the first time in over a century receive the same level of prices for their produce as did their colleagues on the Continent.

Let me now jump ahead to the spring of 1972, when a referendum was finally held on changes in our Constitution that were needed to enable us to join a European Community that had finally agreed to admit Britain, Ireland and also Denmark. This was a hard-fought referendum campaign, marked by many well-attended public meeting throughout the country, addressed mainly by politicians. For the first time in their lives Fianna Fáil and Fine Gael speakers found themselves working side by side, advocating membership, with the case against membership being made on the same platforms by Labour and Official Sinn Féin speakers.

In a country where at the time of accession in 1973 one-quarter of those at work were still engaged in farming, agriculture naturally loomed very large in this debate. Those who favoured joining the Community emphasized that the sharp rise in farm prices in Britain, which would follow the ending of its century-old cheap food policy, would increase Irish farm incomes rapidly. At the same time the opening up of continental markets to our farm produce would also be immensely beneficial. Moreover, the transfer to the EU Budget of the growing burden of farm subsidies would release resources that could then be used to tackle social problems.

The economic argument deployed by opponents of membership concentrated on the likely loss of employment in our heavily protected industries, and on the increases in food prices through the operation of the Common Agricultural Policy. But opponents also drew attention to the fact that, under the Community's recently introduced Common Fishery Policy, the fish off our shores – a resource which, it has to be said, we had up to that time done little to exploit – would have to be shared with the fishermen of other member states.

The outcome of this referendum debate was decisive. A remarkable 70 per cent of the electorate voted, and over four-fifths cast their ballots in favour of membership. And, despite the arguments about job losses in industry and higher food prices, throughout the country a majority of the urban population actually voted for membership.

In retrospect it is now clear that supporters of accession to the Community in 1972 actually seriously underestimated the economic benefits of membership. Thus they failed to foresee the scale of financial transfers to Ireland through the Community Budget, not just to agriculture but also, through newly created EC Structural Funds, to investment in Ireland's very inadequate infrastructure – both in physical assets like roads and public transport and also in human resources, through investment in training schemes.

Most of all there was a notable failure to appreciate the extent to which the opening of continental European markets to Irish-made industrial products would enable Ireland to attract very substantial foreign industrial investment in manufacturing and thus, almost uniquely in Europe, to expand employment in manufacturing and in business services. In the long term this proved to be far more important than either the boost to agriculture or the Structural Fund payments.

In other respects the 1970s was a disturbed decade, for it was marked by two global oil crises. Each of these in turn helped to temporarily boost inflation in Ireland to over 20 per cent. Nevertheless during this decade the benefits the Irish economy received from EC membership reversed for the first time the net outward flow of emigration. During that decade there was an inflow of around 25,000 Irish workers, returning from Britain and bringing their families with them – 100,000 people in all – enough to outweigh the continued outflow of other young people seeking employment abroad. Together with a climbing birth rate, this helped to boost the population by over 400,000 within ten years.

This inflow of workers reflected the fact that, although during the 1970s 20,000 jobs were lost in protected industries, twice as many new and better paid jobs were created by foreign investors in manufacturing sectors such as pharmaceuticals, metals, and machinery – and, in response to these new manufacturing activities, employment in business services almost doubled.

Such was the initial impact on Ireland of accession to the European Community. In the short run, at least, the emphasis placed by supporters of accession on its impact on agriculture had been well justified. Within seven years of accession farm prices had almost quadrupled – reflecting a rapid movement of Irish farm prices up to the much higher EU level, which itself was being increased during that decade. Farm output also increased during this period, albeit neither spectacularly nor very consistently.

In retrospect it might have been better if the early agricultural price increases for Irish farmers had been somewhat less spectacular. For this huge price increase gave rise to a quite excessive level of optimism amongst the farming community. Encouraged by excessively liberal bank lending, this led towards the end of 1970s to a huge jump in land prices and to a boom in the construction of new farm homes and facilities, neither of which could be sustained. Consequently, by 1980 the farm sector found itself, quite unnecessarily, in financial difficulties.

For a few more years the prices of farm products went on rising, but nothing like as rapidly as consumer prices were increasing during the early 1980s. Since then EU policies have just succeeded in maintaining farm prices at about the level of twenty years ago – but in this period consumer prices have almost doubled. That erosion of farm purchasing prices has been only partly compensated by a rise of about one-third in farm output since the early 1980s, with the result that the total purchasing power of farm income is actually lower today than it was in the late 1970s.

Nevertheless, because since the early 1980s the number of people engaged in farming has declined by a further two-fifths, the purchasing power of farm income per person engaged in agriculture has doubled during this period. And this has in fact narrowed somewhat the traditional gap between average incomes in farming and in other activities.

As for the financial transfers through the Community Budget, at the time Ireland joined the EC the scale of these transfers from its Social Fund and from the proposed Regional Fund was also greatly underestimated. From the outset Ireland secured a quite disproportionate share of the Social Fund, which mainly used to develop training on a large scale. At one period Ireland was drawing from the Social Fund resources ten times greater than its proportion of the Community's population. This reflected the fact that the Irish public administration was more effective than those of Southern Europe in devising, and delivering on, schemes to utilize these monies.

In the case of the Regional Fund, Ireland's share was predetermined at the time of its establishment in 1974, being fixed at a figure five times greater than the share our population bore to that of the Community – subject only to the presentation of sufficient suitable projects for financial support – and that was never a problem for Ireland. This pre-allocation of the Regional Fund was based rather crudely upon the population of those areas in member states where output per head was somewhat below the Community average. By securing that for the early decades of membership, the state would be treated as a single region, the danger being that the population of higher-output Dublin would not be included for the purpose of this calculation was avoided.

These two funds later came to be known as the 'Structural Funds', to which was added twenty years later a further fund to assist countries like Ireland that might have difficulties preparing for the introduction of the Euro.

As a result of all this, within five years of accession, EC financial transfers in the form of these Structural Funds, together with subsidies to agriculture under the Common Agricultural Policy, were annually adding a total of 5 per cent to the value of Irish national output, even after deducting Ireland's own contribution to the Community Budget. In today's money terms, by 1978 the amount of these net payments had reached almost two billion Euro a year.

These Structural Fund payments made possible a much larger scale of investment than the Irish state could ever have afforded on its own, both in physical infrastructure, e.g. roads and public transport, and in increasing the productive capacity of Irish workers through training. Whilst these funds did not directly promote economic growth, they removed many bottlenecks that would otherwise have inhibited growth generated by private and public enterprise.

As recently as the early 1990s, these net financial transfers from the EC were still running at 6 per cent of national output. And despite the fact that Irish output per head has since risen above that of the rest of the EC, with the result that we have to contribute a much larger amount to the Community Budget, Ireland nevertheless remains even today a modest net beneficiary of EU membership in terms of the flow of financial resources.

But what has turned out eventually to be of much greater economic importance than either the benefits secured by agriculture or the financial transfers through the Community Budget has, of course, been the impact of the freeing of trade between Ireland and the continental EC countries – opening up this huge market to Irish-made goods.

The underestimation of the gains that would accrue from this process was at least partially a reflection of the fact that both in the 1960s before joining and also during the 1972 referendum campaign, so much attention was concentrated upon the fall in employment that would occur through the withdrawal of industrial protection. Even to many supporters of membership, the certainty of these losses seemed much more real than any potential gains of industrial activity that might arise as a result of multinationals from outside the Community choosing Ireland as a European base. At best that prospect of foreign industrial investment was seen as perhaps offsetting the anticipated losses in the indigenous protected manufacturing sector.

It is true that in the fifteen years before accession the removal of long-standing constraints on foreign investment in Irish manufacturing, as well as the abolition of taxation on profits made from exports, had attracted a number of mainly British and German manufacturers to Ireland. Some, at least, of these British firms were seeking to return to an Irish market from which they had been excluded by restrictive legislation some thirty years earlier, whilst others were attracted by the Anglo-Irish Free Trade Agreement of 1965, which had removed some residual British barriers to Irish exports.

The German investors of that period were mainly seeking to take advantage of the tax relief, although in quite a few cases their proprietors were also trying to get as far away as possible from the possible threat of a war with the Soviet Union, in which the Federal Republic of Germany, because of its proximity to Soviet-occupied East Germany, would be the first to suffer. Indeed this was the reason why the great majority of the mostly small German industries that came to Ireland at that time located in the west of Ireland – two-thirds of them in the climatically favourable south-west!

That earlier phase of external industrial investment had helped to generate economic growth during the period when Ireland was waiting for the lifting of the French veto on British entry so as to allow Britain, and with Britain its economically dependent Irish neighbour, to join the Community.

But investment by most major US multinationals had to await Irish accession to the Community. And the limited scale of earlier British and German investment had given no inkling of the volume of industrial investment that might eventually come from the United States, and to a much lesser extent from Japan and other non-EC countries, once the continental European market had been opened to goods manufactured in Ireland.

The EC requirement that Ireland eliminate tax discrimination favouring exports, as against goods sold in the home market, did not prove a serious deterrent to foreign industrial investment here because the substitution of a 10 per cent flat rate on all manufacturing profits still left Ireland with a clear tax advantage *vis-à-vis* other locations within the Community. Later, in the 1990s, the completion of the Single European Market, which since the mid-1960s had been held up by French objections to the use of qualified majority voting to remove remaining barriers to free and fair trade, gave a further boost to Irish exports to continental EC countries, and thus to external industrial investment in Ireland.

Because of the early benefits of EC membership, in the eight years following accession Irish output rose twice as rapidly as in the rest of the EC, where growth had notably slowed after the first oil crisis of 1974. However, because in the early 1970s our work force was still undereducated, Ireland was not then as attractive a location for external investment in manufacturing as it eventually became. For at the time when Ireland joined the Community the process of expanding our educational system had only recently started, and it was not until the late 1980s that the emergence of a well-educated potential labour force in Ireland complemented the tax relief to an extent that made Ireland a preferred European location for a significant proportion of US industrial investment in Europe.

In the years that followed Ireland's initial, exceptionally successful period of EC membership, economic growth here was halted in its tracks by a self-inflicted wound. This was the need to take urgent and drastic action to avoid a threat of approaching national bankruptcy. Partly perhaps because of the euphoria of early success within the EC, by the late 1970s a combination of hugely excessive spending and the unwise abolition of certain taxes had undermined our public finances. Within four or five years the national debt had been trebled, and by mid-1981 the annual rate of public borrowing was rising towards a totally unsustainable 20 per cent of our national output.

Unhappily, this period in the early 1980s, following the second Oil Crisis of 1979, also saw economic growth in Europe slow to less than 1 per cent a year. This aggravated Ireland's financial crisis by curbing export demand and reducing the flow of industrial investment from the United States.

It was only after growth in Europe resumed in the mid-1980s that foreign industrial investment in Ireland started to recover. After 1993 it helped to boost the Irish growth rate to an astonishing 8 per cent a year – a pace of growth that was maintained until early 2001.

It is worth remarking that in the 1990s exports to countries outside the European Community began to grow twice as fast as those to Britain and to the continental EC countries. What seems to have happened is that the hi-tech base that had been established in Ireland by many multinationals in the earlier period with a view to accessing EC markets had proved sufficiently successful to encourage such firms to also make Ireland a base for the manufacture of goods for export to the rest of the world – half to the United States and half to other countries.

In retrospect, it can be seen that this extension of the export orientation of foreign-owned firms in Ireland helps to account for the scale of demand for Irish labour in Ireland during the 1990s – a demand that was responsible for much of the 8 per cent annual growth of the Irish economy during that decade.

The world outside the EC, which in the early period of Irish EC membership accounted for only one-fifth of our exports, now takes well over one-third of the total export figure. This may be seen as an indirect consequence of Community membership, for if such industries had not initially been sited here in order to access the EC market, Ireland would not now be such a significant base for multinationals exporting to the rest of the world including the United States itself.

This remarkable success of Ireland as a base for manufacturing hi-tech products has been helped by some factors other than the low corporate tax rate and the flow of well-educated young people from an Irish education system that has been transformed since the late 1960s.

To start with Ireland has several natural advantages. The severe cultural loss of Irish as the home language of its people has been compensated in economic terms by the fact that the Irish language was replaced by what was to become the common language of business worldwide, viz. English.

Secondly, we have a well-developed administrative system, and because of past emigration and unemployment Irish people warmly welcome industrial investment. Moreover, the social costs of employment in Ireland are much lower than in continental Europe. And, although up to recently governments have changed fairly frequently, the basic economic policy of the state has been consistently maintained by successive administrations, thus creating a secure basis for foreign investment.

Finally, during the 1990s, a period of transition to full employment, successive national pay agreements involving government, employers, and trade unions, helped to maintain a moderate level of pay increases.

But, had it not been for the opening of the European market to Irish-made products as a result of EC membership, none of these advantages, natural or policy-created, could have produced the kind of economic growth that Ireland has experienced during most of the period since the 1960s – running well ahead of that of the rest of Europe during most of this period. It was the availability of this European market that initially created the scale of demand for labour in Ireland that eventually became such an extraordinary feature of the 1990s.

It has to be said, however, that, but for the happy coincidence of this high labour demand with an exceptional labour supply, this strong demand for labour in Ireland could not have given us a growth rate of more than 4 to 5 per cent a year in the 1990s.

It is this coincidence of demand for and supply of Irish labour in the 1990s that explains the extraordinary 8 per cent annual growth rate of this recent period – a sustained growth rate that has no precedent in Europe, or indeed anywhere else in the developed world.

And it is that development that has enabled Ireland to move within barely a decade from having a level of output per head two-fifths below the European average to a situation in which it now matches the rest of the Community in this respect.

Has there been any economic downside to our membership? Whilst one can argue that the rapidity of the transformation of the Irish economy from by far the poorest in Northern Europe to one of the most prosperous in what is now the European Union has created some social stresses and strains, in purely economic terms it has been almost all sheer gain.

It is true that in order to secure major gains in both agriculture and industry, we had to accept the consequences of the communitarization of fish catches that was affected by the Original Six in 1970 before we joined. However, the special provisions of the EC Fishery Policy that have enabled us to quadruple our catch since the mid-1970s whilst our partners have been required to limit their fishing to the level of almost thirty years ago has softened this blow, and given our total failure to develop this industry before we joined the Community, it is far from clear that we would have been catching more fish today if we had kept control of our fish stocks whilst remaining in relative poverty outside the Community.

The economic balance of membership has been hugely favourable for Ireland – more so, I would think, than for any other member state.

7. Europe, Democracy and Ireland

Larry Siedentop

I want to tell a story about two ways of thinking about democracy, and to do it in connection with the development of the European Union and the membership of countries such as Ireland. In my book *Democracy in Europe* I have argued that there is a crisis of legitimacy in Europe, a crisis that springs from the EU's failure to clarify the nature of its own political project. That is to say, what are the constitutional implications for member states of the acceleration of integration since the late 1980s, an acceleration that was, at least in part, the response of France to the unexpected event of German reunification? The result of this acceleration is that Europe is poised uneasily between confederation and federation. Which is it to be? The Euro project, with its potential for centralizing fiscal as well as monetary policy, seems to point in a federalist direction, while the project for a common security and foreign policy, seems to point in an intergovernmental or confederal direction.

Little wonder that Europeans are confused and often uneasy about the recent and future development of the EU. Public debate in recent years has not done much to dispel this confusion and uneasiness. For it has been dangerously polarized. Those supporting further integration have fallen back on an essentially economic case, urging the advantages of getting richer together – not, you may think, an especially controversial goal. Those opposing further integration have, on the other hand, fallen back on the defence of national sovereignty, an essentially legal category – a category that can be rather sterile and isolationist. In many senses it is anathema to the reasons why Ireland joined the European Community in 1973.

Polarized in this way, public debate has not been very good at informing minds or shaping thinking about the political issues raised by EU development. Nonetheless, I think that the instincts of the public cut deeper than this debate and that the widespread uneasiness is owing to its failure to reach the really crucial issue – which is that of self-government. What is the future of self-government in Europe? Indeed, what are the conditions of self-government in a democratic society on a continental scale? Does the development of the EU threaten to weaken democratic political cultures where they already exist – in the member states – without replacing them elsewhere? That would be disastrous for democracy in Europe. It may well be that the nationalist reactions noticeable in many members states latterly – from Denmark and Holland, through France and Austria, to Italy and Portugal – spring from that fear, though no doubt they are mixed up with other factors as well.

Some commentators speak of a democratic deficit in Europe and assume that it is the same as what I called at the outset a crisis of legitimacy. I do not think that they are the same. Every democratic political system, even the most venerable and apparently successful, is always in deficit. That is because we can always imagine a more democratic process or outcome, a process or outcome that fully engages all the people and elicits their unanimous consent. That is merely to say that democracy is an ideal, a yardstick by which we can measure our own limited successes in that direction. By that yardstick, we always fail, more or less. Yet that very failure is a spur to further effort, to more refined aspiration.

A crisis of legitimacy is different. It arises when there is no widely understood and accepted framework for making the decisions that are going to shape our lives together. It is a sign that there is no demos, no public opinion, no shared view about the stage on which our public lives are to be acted out. That, I suggest, is the dilemma of the EU today after almost half a century of existence. It has created institutions in an ad hoc way and presented itself as primarily an economic undertaking, postponing, if not entirely neglecting, constitutional issues. Of course many of the founding fathers of the EEC were convinced federalists, but the circumstances of early post-war Europe, especially the pariah status of Germany, did not allow them to pursue such a project. Instead they concentrated on the attainable, on economic co-operation that might eventually lay the foundation for federalism. In a sense, that concentration on economic co-operation became too successful. The unprecedented prosperity that it ushered in suggested further steps of economic integration and still further postponement of constitutional clarification.

Europe today is paying the price for such postponement. It is a high price, and it is being paid not only by the member states of the EU but by the applicant states as well. For the delay in establishing anything like the Convention on the Future of Europe means that the difficult, complex issues raised by enlargement have to be settled by an EU that has not yet defined its own political character – an EU that cannot take for granted anything like a consensus across Europe about what should be

done centrally in Brussels and what should remain the preroga-
tives of the member states such as Ireland.

The lack of such a consensus in Europe points to a fundamental difference between the task facing the Founding Fathers
who drew up the American Constitution in Philadelphia in 1787
and the delegates to the European Convention meeting under
former French President, Valéry Giscard d'Estaing. The delegates in Philadelphia had an important shared memory – the
memory of a common subordination to the British Crown, a
subordination which had not seemed unduly oppressive until the
1760s (for the colonies had until then enjoyed great de facto
autonomy). In consequence, the delegates to Philadelphia
tended to see the new federal government as resuming powers
traditionally exercised by the British government. That (British)
ghost at the Convention meant that the delegates were able to
draw upon a pre-existing constitutional sense in drawing up a
new Constitution.

That was an enormous advantage, which Europe does not
enjoy today. Instead, Europe is confronted by the need to build
new institutions and create a constitutional sense at the same
time – in tandem, so to speak. Yet the history of modern Europe
has left an unfortunate legacy in this respect. Projects for unifi-
cation have historically been associated with conquest and dom-
ination – with the ambitions of Napoleon, Hitler and Stalin.
Those associations with empire help to explain the reservations
about European integration in a nation like Britain, which played
an important part in frustrating such continental imperial projects. Those associations continue to raise wider fears about the
prospects for democracy in an integrated Europe, about how
European integration can be combined with self-government
and national political cultures, which remain the primary locus
of democratic habits and attitudes.

These features of the European legacy loom large, I suspect, in the minds of leaders of the applicant countries who have only recently been freed from an empire – the Soviet Empire – and have no wish to return to subjugation. The Irish ought to be especially sympathetic to that concern. For their own rejection of British rule is recent enough and vivid enough to alert them to any risk of a new subjugation. The pity is that such concern about self-government – what is basically a robust and democratically rooted concern – has become confused with the question of national sovereignty. Euro-sceptics in many countries – and that includes a very sizeable minority, at times perhaps even a majority in some applicant countries – have tended to equate the two. They are not the same, for national sovereignty by no means guarantees self-government. And if it is not a sufficient condition, it may not even be a necessary condition. In a sense that was the discovery of American federalism – a political system which not only formally divides sovereignty, but also ensures that much authority and many powers are shared between the centre and periphery.

Clearly, Europe will eventually have to develop a political system, which at least in those very general respects, resembles American federalism. In saying that, I am by no means advocating slavish imitation of American federalism. Europe ought gradually to create a political system which serves its own needs, respects its own traditions and can elicit consent from its diverse peoples.

There are at least three conditions that any successful democratic political system has to satisfy. First, it must be readily intelligible. Second, it must be able to mobilize and shape opinion – that is, educate; and third, it must entertain, providing some public theatre. By those tests, I'm afraid it is clear that the European Union has a long way to go. Europe has to face up to

this formidable task – and the Convention on the Future of
Europe is a sign that the EU has, belatedly, come to recognize
that fact. It is vitally important that the EU also recognizes the
dimensions of the challenge facing it. It should not try to go for
a quick fix, in which constitutional clarification becomes simply
the latest example of a technocratic mind-set that is inclined to
build from the top down, neglecting the informal habits and attitudes that are the heart of any political culture. For if not rooted
in habits and attitudes, a European Constitution could be a life-
less thing, a thing that has no hold over people and might even
contribute to their being manipulated. After all, the Soviet
Union also had a Constitution ...

So constitutional clarification should not be approached as a
merely technical matter – as a formal exercise in distributing
competences to different agencies. It is above all about the
European Union beginning to acquire a hold over minds and
hearts, something that it has had only a limited success in doing
up to now.

It is partly a question of generations. I have been very struck,
when travelling around European capitals in the last year or two,
by a discrepancy between the attitudes of different age groups.
My impression is that intense Euro-enthusiasm and intense
Euro-scepticism are both largely confined to the middle-aged.
The young, and Ireland is a very good case in point, are different. They take many of the changes accomplished in recent
decades in European civil society – such as free movement of
persons, goods and capital associated with the creation of a single market – for granted. They can hardly imagine Europe otherwise – which is to say that they don't feel enormous gratitude
to the European Union as the means of having brought about
many of these changes.

Now I think that phenomenon is instructive. It tells us about one way of thinking about democracy, and its limitations. It is a way of thinking illustrated by some of the public argument in the run-up to the first Irish referendum on Nice. Voters were almost invited to express their preferences as consumers, to concentrate on the matters that are 'nearest home'. Such an attitude towards voting reveals the terrible limitations of the market-place, and, by implication, of all public arguments founded merely on economic incentives, on the pursuit of self-interest. They appeal to us merely as we are – with our current preoccupations – our day-to-day preferences – our habits as consumers. They do not tap our aspirations to be something more than consumers, our aspirations to be citizens, active members of the public realm.

That sense of counting in the public sphere, of having some weight as a citizen, was immediate and palpable in the form of government that gave birth to the idea of democracy – the *polis* or city-state of the ancient world. The small scale of organization made the ideal of an equal distribution of power or influence among citizens seem not beyond reach. The difficulty of extending that ideal to a political organization on the scale of the nation-state has proved a central theme of European history from the sixteenth to the twentieth century. Only slowly and precariously have the nation-states been able to give their citizens a sense of empowerment, enabling them to see the law as in some sense their own work. That sense, which I call a 'culture of consent', is, in the nature of things, fragile. And the greatest political risk attached to the progress of European integration and the development of the European Union is that the centralizing of power without being replaced at any other level, so hard won in the nation-states, might weaken such cultures.

It was such a perception that for centuries led political thinkers such as Montesquieu to conclude that a political system on a continental or quasi-continental scale could only be run in one way — that is, tyrannically or despotically. It was only after the nineteenth century with the success of American federalism that the earlier pessimistic assumption began to give way to a more optimistic scenario, one which held out the hope of democracy on a continental scale. Why should Europe not match the success of American federalism in creating a culture of consent that would overcome the national rivalries that had plunged the continent into disastrous war twice in half a century?

If Europe is to develop such a culture of consent, then it must first begin to foster a constitutional sense. Such a sense is the prerequisite of a European demos, a coherent public opinion across Europe. It would be foolish and even dangerous to pretend that such a demos exists today. I'm afraid that the creation of the European Parliament has not succeeded in fostering a demos across Europe. The European Parliament has very little hold over opinion at best. At worst its existence can even smack of pseudo-democracy — with low and declining turnouts at elections, as well as parliamentarians who often have almost no public profile. Certainly the European Parliament has not begun to create the kind of open political class across Europe which, in the longer run, is the only alternative to a technocratic Europe governed by bureaucrats.

I say these somewhat sombre things to illustrate the formidable challenge facing the Convention on the Future of Europe. Moreover, I say them in order to identify the risks posed by such a Convention at this stage of Europe's development. The principal risk is that the Convention may be tempted to be too ambitious. Its great object ought, in my view, to be not to write an over-elaborate Constitution but to take steps that begin to foster a constitutional sense. If the Convention is too ambitious it risks — quite apart from having its work rejected or modified out of recognition at a subsequent inter-governmental conference – producing a document that becomes a dead letter on the one hand, or leads to the judicializing of the European process through constant appeals to the Luxembourg Court on the other.

Neither of those outcomes would create a culture of consent or the European demos that such a culture presupposes. By contrast, the early reports from the Convention suggest one proposal that could mark the first plausible step towards creating a demos, a Europe-wide opinion that supplements but does not supplant national opinions. That is the proposal that a right of exit from the European Union be enshrined in a constitutional treaty. Such a right – no doubt hedged round by conditions – would immediately establish a difference between the new political system in Europe and American federalism. It would establish that while Europe may have become more than a confederation of nation-states, it has no intention of becoming a federation on the American model. For the Civil War in the United States resulted in the union becoming indissoluble, with the states denied the right to secede.

The fact that the Convention coincides with the moment of EU enlargement makes such a right of exit absolutely indispensable. For no one really knows what the enlarged Union will be like or how it will operate. Whether the existing degree of central regulation in the name of a single market can be sustained must be an open question. And the attempt to reconstruct the relationship between the central EU institutions – the Commission, the Parliament and the Council system – may be undone or prove futile in the face of pressures generated by a Union of up to twenty-five member states. The attractions of creating a larger democratic and prosperous Europe, as well as the moral obligations created in more than a decade of negotiations between applicant states and the current Union, have to be viewed together with their downside, a possible partial deconstruction of the EU in its present form. Only one thing is clear. The future will not be like the present.

It may, with luck and skill, be possible for the Convention to make progress in three other areas – areas that could begin to foster a constitutional sense. The first and probably most difficult is a clearer separation of legislative and executive powers at the centre, which raises especially the issue of the relations between the Commission and a Council system in which legislative and executive functions are combined. Those relations are at the mercy of the very different ambitions of small and large states, with the former looking to a stronger Commission and the latter preferring to strengthen the Council in order to promote an intergovernmental model.

Two other areas ought to prove easier for the Convention: human rights and bicameralism. Unfortunately, the development of a rights-based political culture in Europe is currently rather jeopardized by the proposal to attach the new European Charter of Rights to a constitutional treaty. Although the new Charter would not be strictly comparable in its application to the long-standing European Convention on Human Rights, the existence of two such sources of rights litigation does not serve the cause of simplicity or easy comprehension. The scope of the new Charter also lends itself to the charge that it inflates the language of rights, turning what may well be desirable, if somewhat controversial, social and economic goals into rights. The American experience suggests that a relatively short list of rights may do more to foster a rights-based political culture. The existence of two rights documents could, moreover, lead to conflicts of jurisdiction between the Strasbourg and Luxembourg courts, further muddling the public mind and so perhaps delaying the emergence of a rights-based consensus across the European Union.

The third area in which progress is possible may be the most important. For it touches directly the purpose of holding a Convention on the Future of Europe. In my view a European Senate, an upper house consisting of leading national politicians elected by their respective legislatures and retaining a national political role, is indispensable if Europe is to begin to foster a constitutional sense. Such a Senate ought to have a limited agenda, and concern itself especially with the issue of subsidiarity – of who decides what. It ought to have the right to review and, if need be, veto proposed new European initiatives, as well as the right to reconsider powers already vested in Brussels – applying rigorously the test of whether something is better done at the national level or centrally. Such a Senate ought to bring to bear a presumption against extending central power unless the advantages of doing so are unambiguous.

Some will argue that the last thing Europe needs is a new institution. That is a mistaken view, for at least two reasons. The first reason is that such a Senate would be the best way of conciliating a territorial principle and a population principle across the Union. Those two principles, their competition and reconciliation, are necessary in anything like a democratic political system on a continental scale. A Senate in which the territorial principle was favoured and enabled to constrain the population or majority principle, would do much to reassure the smaller member states – as well as reconnecting national political classes with the European project, something that is desperately needed. For it is almost as if the existence of the European Parliament has served as an excuse for national political classes to distance themselves from the project.

The other reason for creating a Senate is even more compelling. Such a body would become, in effect, a permanent constitutional convention – debating and shaping opinion across the

continent, through its closer connection with national legislatures and national political classes, on central questions about
the nature and purposes of the European Union. Only such a
body could both reflect and direct opinion about who should
decide what in Europe, about the limits that integration ought to
respect. A permanent, ongoing debate conducted by a body like
the Senate, representing national political classes, could hold the
attention of European peoples and begin to create a culture of
consent and a demos.

I began this essay by referring to two ways of thinking about
democracy. The first, which I have already explored, takes an
economist's view, and sees the democratic process as something
like the market-place – with parties, by analogy with companies, competing for consumer preferences. Satisfying people's
wants rather than changing them is the central question. I have
suggested that this was up to a point a model for understanding
the first Irish referendum on Nice, when neither government
nor parties were emphatic enough about the really important
question before the electorate – the question of what served a
common European interest, the European public weal.

That question became far more central in the run-up to the
second referendum. And that is the question that an alternative
way of thinking about democracy – a way that goes back at least
as far as Jean-Jacques Rousseau in the eighteenth century –
makes absolutely central to the democratic process. Only when
political institutions lead people to put aside, at least temporarily,
their own interests and preferences in order to consider instead
what promotes or serves the common interest does democracy
work as it ought to do. The democratic process, properly understood, changes people. It lifts them from being merely consumers to being citizens, taking a different view of their own
interests in relation to the interests of others. Democracy does

not turn us into saints. At its best and at the margins, it can help to moralize us, lifting our horizons.

It is often argued the much of Ireland's spectacular economic development, especially over the last decade, owes much to its membership of the European Union over the last thirty years. Now, at this point of further enlargement within its membership, the Union would in turn do well to look at the message sent from the electorate by the outcome of the first Nice referendum in Ireland.

A formidable challenge now faces the European Union. By neglecting its constitutional identity in favour of an economic identity in the past, it has failed to arouse and sustain idealism in the way that a democratic political system can do. That is why it often receives less gratitude than it deserves. With the help of the Convention on the Future of Europe, it must now change its ways and begin to foster a constitutional sense to which people feel greater attachment and belonging.

8. Ireland and Europe: Embracing Change

Bertie Ahern

The European Union is perhaps the greatest success story in the relations between free democratic countries. It is a model of political and economic cooperation that has no precedent in world history. It has built peace and prosperity in Europe. It will, by 2004, be more than four times the size of its original membership and will stretch from the Atlantic to the Danube and from the Arctic Circle to the Mediterranean. With the United States and Japan, it is a key motor of the world's economy.

What the European Union says and does is important and it does matter. And for us in Ireland it matters a great deal. Over the course of the last year, the Irish people had an opportunity to discuss and reflect on our membership of the European Union. Our debate was unique among EU members. It was also timely. In our referendum process we addressed the key issues regarding our relationship with Europe. And in the end the Irish people convincingly decided to approve the Nice Treaty and open the way for enlargement of the Union. In so doing we also made sure that Ireland remained at the heart of Europe.

We have become increasingly comfortable and familiar with the Union of the present. But we know the Union of the future will have a different shape and present new challenges, as well as opportunities.

Our ability to adapt to the Union as it emerges and develops will determine our future prosperity and success. A Union of twenty-five member states, or more, will be very different from a Union of fifteen. It will have a far greater population, be more diverse and have significantly different levels of economic development among its members. But although more complex, it will be a Union from which we will have nothing to fear and to which we can continue to contribute, and gain, a great deal.

This, therefore, is a time for creative thought and careful assessment. Membership of the EU has been central to Ireland's interests for the last thirty years. We are seen by many as the shining example of how membership can benefit a small, peripheral, underdeveloped country. We have successfully integrated our economy, our currency and many other aspects of our lives with our European partners.

Not being part of Europe is, frankly, unthinkable. It is, to quote the late Taoiseach Jack Lynch, like 'the choice faced by Robinson Crusoe when the ship came to bring him back into the world again'.

But what of the Union of the future? Even as Europe changes, our principles and goals, as Europeans and Irish people, are constant. They are:

A Europe at peace.

A Europe of strong individual member states but where sovereignty continues to be shared where it makes sense to do so.

A Europe of balanced institutional arrangements that serve the interests of all member states, big and small.

A Europe of quality and solidarity that works for all its citizens.

A Europe that contributes effectively to progressive developments in the rest of the world.

And an Ireland that is committed to Europe and plays its part to the fullest.

As our Union develops, I want Ireland to be there, ready to lead, not to drop behind. I want us to continue to assert ourselves with confidence – confident as Irish and European men and women.

Ireland's relationship with Europe is multi-layered and complex. It is a relationship that has changed from decade to decade and often from year to year. For much of its history, Europe, in Irish eyes, was our best hope of securing assistance in establishing our independence. Over the centuries, Europe was a source of hope and sustenance. During the time of the penal laws, vital elements of our national heritage were preserved in the Irish colleges scattered across the continent, in Paris, Louvain, Salamanca and Rome.

In the nineteenth century our cultural and language revival was greatly assisted by European thinkers. In every century prior to our independence, European political ideas and models, be they the French Revolution, the Young Italy movement or the nationalist aspirations within the dual Austro-Hungarian monarchy, provided hope and inspiration to advocates of Irish freedom.

Indeed, when talks opened in Brussels in January 1962 on Ireland's first application to join the Common Market, Taoiseach Seán Lemass was quick to stress that Ireland was a part of the European family of nations. In a speech to the ministers of the Community member states, he said on 18 January:

Ireland belongs to Europe by history, tradition and sentiment no less than by geography. Our destiny is bound up with that of Europe and our outlook and our way of life have, for fifteen centuries, been moulded by the Christian ideals and the intellectual and cultural values on which European civilization rests. Our people have always tended to look to Europe for inspiration, guidance and encouragement.[1]

Despite these comments, Seán Lemass would have been keenly aware that Ireland upon achieving independence did not adopt, as might have been expected, European models of governance and law. This reflected both an understandable concern amongst politicians of all persuasions with stabilizing and establishing the state institutions. It also reflected the fact that Europe was a very unstable place in the first two-and-a-half decades of our independence. A continent divided by political instability and war was not attractive to us. It was through the construction of genuine European institutions that Europe broke with its past and managed to escape the vicious cycle of war and distrust.

Ireland in the late 1950s was in a dismal economic state. Emigration had driven the population of the country below three million. This exodus, combined with low levels of economic and social investment, led to poor economic progress. Third-level education was restricted to a small élite. A full second-level education was available only to the lucky minority. Ireland was reaching the very limits of viability as a state.

Faced with the economic reality of the late 1950s, Ireland began to open its economy to the broader world and open its political system to the radical political developments taking place in Europe. We abandoned our policy of economic isolation, based as it was on high levels of economic protection. We abandoned it because it had failed and offered no hope for the future.

Our best hope for the future lay in the emerging EEC. After

two failed attempts, Ireland was admitted to the European Union in 1973. It was a defining moment for our country. The people's decision to join the EEC was the right choice. It was a great vote of confidence in our ability to make our way in the new Europe and to move out from the shadow of our nearest neighbour. It set our country firmly on the right road to progress, prosperity and full employment.

On a personal level, I have strong memories of the referendum on European accession. It was the first political campaign in which I canvassed and engaged in debate. I remember well the strong case we made for Europe. We said that we were joining with the Community to support the fundamental idea of uniting Europe to prevent war and to bring people closer together in closer harmony. We also said that joining the EEC would help eliminate unemployment, attract foreign investment, open new markets and raise living standards. We were right.

There is complete agreement that the thirty years since we joined the EU have been years of unprecedented and rapid change. It has seen liberation in terms of economic circumstances. It has seen a massive improvement in both the duration and quality of life of our citizens. It has seen an opening up of opportunities that would have been unimaginable forty years ago.

Our economic performance since 1987 has been staggering by any standards. Clearly our own national efforts were the primary cause of that progress. But the framework of the European Union in terms of the single market, in terms of the substantial funding provided and, above all, in terms of the political and economic stability Europe provides, were, and are, absolutely vital to our success.

Ireland has been very much at the forefront of the EU's progress. We were strong supporters of the single market and we are of course in the first wave of countries to participate in the single currency. And it is very clear that we strongly support the enlargement of the Union which lies ahead.

The EU is about a set of shared values of democracy, respect for human rights and the rule of law. These are values that Ireland has helped to shape. The recent successfully concluded negotiations at the Copenhagen Summit mean the applicant countries from Eastern and Central Europe will now take their rightful place among the nations.

For any of us around long enough to remember the Soviet invasion of Hungary, the Prague Spring in 1968, or the imposition of a military dictatorship in Poland in 1981, the transformation of these countries from totalitarianism to democracy, from oppression to freedom, and from a society governed by powerful élites to a society governed by the rule of law, marks a brave new chapter in the history of this continent.

Europe has ensured that national disputes, national envies, national wants can be regulated and moderated and that compromises that serve the interests of all can be built. It is this spirit of compromise, as much as the unique institutional structures of the European Union, that has been the glue that has held the Union together. For the Union to continue to prosper, this spirit of compromise must also continue. It is a spirit based on trust and solidarity and nourished by mutual self-interest. It means, for instance, that Ireland, while pursuing a policy of military neutrality, has actively worked with partners to develop an effective and principled foreign policy for the Union.

The Union has prospered by creating a framework for a working market economy on a European scale. But Europe has also created the conditions for enhanced social standards. Rather than following each other in a race to the bottom, these standards have been stabilized and raised across the Union.

Designing Europe's shape and possibilities did not, and could not, stop with the Treaty of Nice. Heads of state and government accepted at Nice that we would have to take on the challenge of how we managed and organized our work in the context of a Union of twenty-five members or more. Clearly, significant change was required. This challenge is being taken forward through the vitally important work of the Convention on the Future of Europe, at which governments are represented but which also includes representatives from national parliaments, the European Commission and the European Parliament.

After the Convention finishes its work, the governments will meet together in an Intergovernmental Conference to agree a new Treaty. Obviously the Report of the Convention, which was produced in mid-2003, was a highly influential starting point for the work of the Intergovernmental Conference. The new Treaty that will emerge at the end of this work is being referred to by many as a 'Constitutional Treaty'. Whatever its final title – and I am not unduly exercised by titles – this Treaty will be of vital interest to each and every member state and the citizens of Europe. Getting it right is crucial.

Designing a Union that works effectively and a Union that is more democratic and accountable is what we are about. Ireland has, from the outset, been fully engaged in and is playing an active part in this process. We are working to ensure that Ireland's essential interests and values are reflected in the Convention's outcome.

There is little doubt that a never-ending circle of treaty change would not be in Europe's interest. It is essential, therefore, that the new Treaty for Europe, when it emerges, serves our Union well into the future. This will require a significant consolidation and revision of the existing treaties.

The European Union has shown itself to be visionary, yet sensible. Dynamic, yet sensitive. Ireland has never been a spectator as Europe changes. We were and are an intrinsic part of the design team.

The question is: what change? And how are we to be guided in weighing up the various proposals for change and reform? The issues that arise are important for all member states, big and small, old and new. From its very beginning, it was always clear that Europe would not be made all at once or according to a single plan. It was always understood that it would be built through concrete achievements. This indeed is the way in which the Union as we know it today has emerged. But I believe that we can now begin to see the shape of the Union of the future more clearly than was perhaps possible in the past.

As we work with our EU partners to craft a new Treaty, we will, like others, strongly defend our core national interests. On issues of principle we will be firm. On all matters of practicalities and organization, we will be open-minded and flexible.

For Ireland, Europe has always been more than an economic arrangement. Seán Lemass, the great modernizer of Irish politics, was unambiguous in his desire to see Ireland play a full part in the development of the Community at all levels. If the European Union is to thrive in the future it must prove itself capable of tackling the range of challenges facing the new Europe. These are challenges of such a scale that no member state can hope to tackle them on its own. For example, we all share the desire to protect the interests of the European Union and its citizens from cross-border criminal activity.

There are many issues arising at the Convention that cannot adequately be addressed in the context of these remarks. The Minister for Foreign Affairs has recently set out the government's position on all of these in considerable detail. However, I would like to touch on one or two areas that are obviously of particular importance.

Europe must meet the needs of its citizens. The European Union has been a success because it has worked for the benefit of its peoples. It has not been a success by accident. It has worked in particular through creating a space for peace, political democracy, and freedom. It is the ground spring of public support in every member state that sustains the Union. We must ensure that this support is developed and deepened.

What we want to ensure most of all is that, as Europe develops, it does so transparently and in a manner faithful to its ideals. It is important to remember throughout that we are not in the process of building a new Europe. We are in the process of building on five decades of successful European integration. That process of integration has been built on the twin pillars of respect for the national identities of the member states and the construction of European institutions that serve the European interest. Clearly the Treaty that we are seeking to achieve will build on these two essential pillars.

It is essential that Europe has the best and most effective institutions. Ireland will, therefore, be very open to institutional reforms that equip the Union to do its job. We will not be dogmatic on the detail, so long as the principles of equality and balance are respected. And as we make our institutions more effective, we must also try to ensure that their democratic legitimacy is strengthened.

Thus, for example, we can see the real merits of having an elected President of the European Commission, and in strengthening the European Parliament's role across a range of areas. National parliaments themselves also need to be given greater weight in the workings of the Union. We are considering closely the important proposals that have been put forward recently by the Commission, by the Benelux countries, by France and Germany jointly, and by many other partners.

Ireland also has made its own distinctive contribution to this process, for example, calling for National Parliaments to have a role in ensuring the Union does not exceed its function in relation to matters best dealt with by national governments. We have argued trenchantly and submitted specific proposals to protect citizens' rights in dealing with the institutions of the Union. In the work of the Convention and the debates across Europe, there is little support for a radical extension of the Union's functions. Europe should do what Europe does best.

The member states, for their part, should co-operate to their mutual advantage, but remain in the driving seat in other areas. There is little talk of bringing to Brussels areas of internal policy that are not already there. There is, for instance, little support for an EU-wide tax to fund a radical expansion of the EU budget. Nor is it envisaged that the EU would assume a major role in the areas of health care or education. The government firmly believes that such an expansion is unnecessary at this time.

In a Union of almost thirty states, only the most exceptional areas of European Union policy and legislation should be subject to the requirement of unanimity in decision-making. We have always strongly supported the extension of qualified-majority voting to areas where it can help to increase the effectiveness of decision-making. But, clearly, there are also a limited number of red line areas where unanimity must continue to apply if the decisions of the Union are to have legitimacy with its citizens. Amendments to the Treaties, taxation and, of course, decisions on security and defence are examples of areas where unanimity must be maintained.

As I said earlier on, change is inevitable. And, let me make it very clear: we are advocates of such change. What is important is that this is change for the better. An EU that does not work well is of little value to any of its people. Our citizens would very quickly complain if Europe could not make the decisions and adopt the policies that allow it to respond and adapt to changing circumstances.

We are determined to negotiate positive change and reform of the EU. I do not wish to minimize the challenge to Ireland of the negotiations that lie ahead. Nor do I wish to exaggerate them. But Ireland approaches the agenda on the future of Europe with confidence in our ability to progress our interests and play a creative and constructive role in shaping Europe's future.

We also do so with the firm intention that, just as the EU is seeking to renew itself through the work of the Convention, we too must begin to re-energize and upgrade our national approach to the Union. After thirty years of membership it is time that we do so. We are no longer the 'poor kid on the block'. What worked in the past may no longer be what is required to meet our new circumstances.

Ireland will hold the Presidency of the European Union for the first six months of 2004. It is a function that we have performed in the past with great success. We have for some time been working to ensure that our preparations for this are fully in place. We are actively consolidating our relationships with the existing member states, and further developing and expanding our contacts with the prospective new members.

It will be during our presidency that the applicant states become members on 1 May 2004. This will be a day of truly historic significance and celebration. We will proudly chair the Union as it embarks on a new and exciting chapter in its development. As we move closer to the date of enlargement, there is a new energy within the European Union. There are new languages being spoken. New faces. More seats around the table. While they are not yet full members, the applicant countries are already making their presence felt.

Together, we are about to embark on an exciting journey of change. Since its foundation, and certainly since Ireland joined in 1973, the European Union has been prepared to take brave steps into uncharted territory. Those who innovate and experiment, however well they prepare the ground, accept that success is not guaranteed. With venture comes some risk.

Every enlargement, every new initiative, every change in emphasis or new departure in the Union's history has required a measure of boldness and ambition. With every step we have embraced challenge and opportunity together. Through flexibility, and a willingness to adapt to meet new circumstances, we have enabled ourselves to build success upon success. We have achieved great things for our people. The same convictions and principles should guide us forward now.

Since our people voted overwhelmingly to join the then EEC in 1973, we have fought our corner and defended our interests. Our people, while strongly supportive of our membership, have not been afraid to raise their voices to make their concerns known. They have made it clear that they cannot and will not be taken for granted.

But, at the same time, we in Ireland have always kept the bigger picture in firm view. In engaging with all the routine work of membership, we have always been able to lift our eyes to recall the fundamental truth: what is good for Europe has been good for Ireland. What we have invested has been returned to us one-hundred fold. As we have worked shoulder to shoulder with our partners, we have prospered and developed together. So we should not be scared of change now. We should believe in our own ability to manage change and drive it forward.

I referred earlier to the vision the late Jack Lynch and Seán Lemass had of Europe and our place in it. That vision was inspired by a very different Ireland. I too have my vision of

Europe which I believe is grounded in TODAY's Ireland. It's a vision of a Europe that is not just an economic entity but one that has a strong social dimension.

I believe the European Union is THE model for the regulation of economic globalization. It's the key defence mechanism against any race to the bottom in terms of social standards. It's the model that has seen rich member states facilitating rather than preventing the catch-up of less-developed countries such as the Ireland of thirty years ago and the applicant states of today. It is a model that goes far beyond free trade and constrains the naked use of economic and diplomatic power. It's a model that is law-based and consensual. That model is, I believe, one with which today's Ireland strongly identifies.

I am confident that the process we are now engaged in will ensure that the European Union continues to develop in ways that we can welcome, and support. It will be more democratic and transparent. It will be more effective. And its purpose and scope will be more easily understood by the citizens of Europe. In short, I believe that it will be a Union of which we in Ireland, and all of Europe, will be proud to be a part.

Notes

INTRODUCTION

1. *Irish Times*, 22 November 1990.
2. H. Lefebvre, *The Production of Space*, trans. D. Nicholson-Smith (Massachusetts 1991).

1. THE DYNAMICS OF MEMBERSHIP
JIM HOURIHANE

1. Robert Malthus, *Essay on the Principle of Population*, (1817).
2. T. Ryle Dwyer, *Nice Fellow – A Biography of Jack Lynch* (Cork 2001).

2. CHANGING TIMES, CHANGING CULTURES
MICHAEL CRONIN

1. Geoffrey Taylor, *The Emerald Isle* (London 1952), p. 141.
2. Paul Virilio, *Vitesse et Politique* (Paris 1977).
3. Central Statistics Office, *That Was Then, This Is Now* (Dublin 2000), p. 58.
4. Joe Cleary, 'Modernization and Aesthetic Ideology' in Ray Ryan (ed.), *Writing in the Irish Republic: Literature, Culture, Politics 1949–1999* (London 2000), p. 207.
5. Donal Murphy, 'Introduction', *That Was Then, This Is Now*, pp. 5–6.
6. Sean D. Barrett, 'Policy Changes, Output Growth and Investment in Irish Tourism 1986–1996', *Irish Banking Review* (Autumn 1997), 39–48.
7. James Joyce, *Ulysses* (Harmondsworth 1971), p. 13.

8. C. Freeman, 'Preface to Part II' in G. Dosi, C. Freeman, R. Nelson, G. Silverberg and I. Soete, *Technical Change and Economic Theory* (London 1988).

9. Emer Sheerin, 'Heritage Centres' in Michel Peillon and Eamon Slater (eds), *Encounters with Modern Ireland* (Dublin 1998), pp. 39–48.

10. Régis Debray, *Introduction à la Médiologie* (Paris 2000), p.200.

11. Tom Garvin, 'The Quiet Revolution: The Remaking of Irish Political Culture' in Ray Ryan (ed.), *Writing in the Irish Republic: Literature, Culture, Politics 1949–1999* (London 2000), p. 200.

12. Geraldine Moane, 'Colonialism and the Celtic Tiger: Legacies of History and the Quest for Vision' in Peadar Kirby, Luke Gibbons and Michael Cronin (eds), *Reinventing Ireland: Culture, Society and the Global Economy* (London 2002), p. 110.

13. Ulrich Beck, *Risk Society: Towards a New Modernity* (London 1992).

3. IRISH AND EUROPEAN LAW
CATHRYN COSTELLO

1. *O'Nuallain*, 1999 No 154 JR (Ir. HCt., 2 July 1999).

2. *Watson v. The Environmental Protection Agency* [2002] 2 IR 454.

3. For example, *Maher v. Minister for Agriculture, Food and Rural Development* [2001] 2 IR 139; *Duff v. Minister for Agriculture and Food* [1999] I.E.H.C. 190.

4. Council Directive 75/117/EEC of 10 February 1975 on the approximation of the laws of the member states relating to the application of the principle of equal pay for men and women [1975] OJ L45/198; Council Directive 76/207/EEC of 9 February 1976 on the implementation of the principle of equal treatment for men and women as regards access to employment, vocational training and promotion, and working conditions [1976] OJ L39/40 ('the Equal Treatment Directive'); Council Directive 79/7/EEC of 19 December 1978 on the progressive implementation of the principle of equal treatment for men and women in matters of social security [1979] OJ L6/24; Council Directive 86/378/EEC of 24 July 1986 on the implementation of the principle of equal treatment for men and women in occupational social security schemes [1986] OJ L225/40; Council Directive 86/613/EEC of 11 December 1986 on the

application of the principle of equal treatment for men and women engaged in an activity, including agriculture, in a self-employed capacity, and on the protection of self-employed women during pregnancy and motherhood [1986] OJ L359/56; Council Directive 92/85/EEC of 19 October 1992 on the introduction of measures to encourage improvements in the safety and health at work of pregnant workers or workers who have recently given birth or are breastfeeding [1992] OJ L348/1; Council Directive 96/34/EC of 3 June 1996 on the framework agreement on parental leave concluded by UNICE, CEEP and the ETUC [1996] OJ L145/11, eventually agreed to by the United Kingdom in Council Directive 97/75/EC of 15 December 1997 amending and extending, to the United Kingdom of Great Britain and Northern Ireland, Directive 96/34/EEC on the framework agreement on parental leave concluded by UNICE, CEEP and the ETUC [1997] OJ L10/24; Council Directive 97/80/EC of 15 December 1997 on the burden of proof in cases of discrimination based on sex [1998] OJ L14/6, eventually accepted by the United Kingdom in Council Directive 98/52/EC of 13 July 1998 on the extension of Directive 97/80/EC on the burden of proof in cases of discrimination based on sex to the United Kingdom of Great Britain and Northern Ireland [1998] OJ L205/66.

5. Council Directive 2000/43/EC of 29 June 2000 implementing the principle of equal treatment between persons irrespective of racial or ethnic origin [2000] OJ L180/22 and Council Directive 2000/78/EC of 27 November 2000 establishing a general framework for equal treatment in employment and occupation [OJ2000] OJ L303/16.

6. See for example, Parliament and Council Regulation 1592/2002 EC of 15 July 2002 on common rules in the field of civil aviation and establishing a European Aviation Safety Agency [2002] OJ L240/1–21; Parliament and Council Directive 97/13/EC of 10 April 1997 on a common framework for general authorizations and individual licences in the field of telecommunications services [1997] OJ L117/15.

7. Alan Dashwood, 'States in the European Union' (1998), 23 *E.L.Rev.* 201, 213.

8. Robert Dahl, *Democracy and its Critics* (Yale 1989), p. 339.

9. David Held, *Democracy and the Global Order* (Cambridge and Oxford 1995), pp. 16–17.

10. Article 292 (ex 219) EC.

11. Keeping constituent states to their bargains is a central task in any divided power system. As the famous US jurist Oliver Wendel Holmes opined, 'I do not think the United States would come to an end if we lost our power to declare an Act of Congress void. I do think the Union would be imperilled if we could not make that declaration as to the laws of the several states.' Oliver Wendell Holmes, *Collected Legal Papers* (1920), pp. 295–6.

12. Case 26/62 *Van Gend en Loos v. Nederlandse Administratie der Belastingen* [1963] ECR 1.

13. Case 6/64 *Costa v. ENEL* [1964] ECR 1141; Case 11/70 *Internationale Handelsgesellschaft* [1970] ECR 1125; Case 106/77 *Amministrazione delle Finanze dello Stato v. Simmenthal* [1978] ECR 629.

14. Case 29/69 *Stauder v. City of Ulm* [1969] ECR 419; Case 11/70 *Internationale Handelsgesellschaft* [1970] ECR 1125 and subsequent cases.

15. The German Constitutional Court ruled in 1974 in Solange I that 'in the hypothetical case of conflict between Community law … and the … fundamental rights in the [German] Constitution … the Constitution prevails …' [1974] 2 CMLR 540, 549–550. However, by 1986 in Solange II, it had largely accepted that the protection of fundamental rights at EC level was sufficient. It stated, 'So long as the European Communities, and in particular the caselaw of the European Court, generally ensure an effective protection of fundamental rights as against the sovereign powers of the Communities … the … Constitutional Court will no longer exercise its jurisdiction … to review such legislation by the standard of the fundamental rights contained in the German Constitution.' [1987] 3 CMLR 225, 265.

16. See Paul Craig, 'United Kingdom Sovereignty after *Factortame*' (1991) 11, *YEL*, 221.

17. For example, a remedy in damages against the state for 'sufficiently serious' breaches of Community law. See Case C-6 & 9/90 *Francovich and Bonifaci v. Italy* [1991] ECR I-5357.

18. J.H.H. Weiler, 'The Transformation of Europe', *Yale Law Journal*, 100 (1991), 2415.

19. Article 119 EEC, now, after amendment Article 141 EC.

20. Case 149/77 *Defrenne v. S.A.B.E.N.A.* [1978] ECR 1635.

21. See, for example, *McDermott and Cotter v. Minister for Social Welfare* [1987] I.L.R.M. 324.

22. 'No provision of the Constitution invalidates laws enacted, acts done or measures adopted by the State which are necessitated by the obligations of membership or prevents [EU law] from having force of law in the State.'

23. Seamus Henchy, 'The Irish Constitution and the EEC' (1977) 12 Duke L.J. 20, 23.

24. Diarmuid Rossa Phelan, *Revolt or Revolution – The Constitutional Boundaries of the European Community* (Dublin 1997).

25. Neil MacCormick, 'The Maastricht-Urteil: Sovereignty Now' *ELJ*, 1 (1995), 259.

26. De Witte, 'Community Law and National Constitutional Values', *L.I.E.I.*, 2 (1991), 22.

27. Parliament and Council Directive 2003/15/EC of 27 February 2003 amending Council Directive 76/768/EEC on the approximation of the laws of the member states relating to cosmetic products [2003] OJ L66/26.

28. *Meagher v. Minister for Agriculture* [1994] 1, I.L.R.M. 1. For critiques of the decision see Anthony Whelan, casenote (1993), DULJ 152; Gerard Hogan and Anthony Whelan, *Ireland and the European Union: Constitutional and Statutory Texts and Commentary* (Dublin 1995), pp. 51–67.

29. *Maher v. Minister for Agriculture, Food and Rural Development* [2001] 2, IR 139.

30. Gerard Hogan and Alex Schuster, 'Ireland' in Jurgen Schwarze (ed.), *Administrative Law under European Influence* (Baden-Baden, Germany 1996).

31. Advocates Generals Opinions on the Charter include AG Alber, 1 February 2001 in Case C-340/99 TNT Traco [2001], ECR I-4109; AG Tizzano, 8 February 2001, Case C-173/99 BECTU [2001] ECR I-4881; AG Mischo, 22 February 2001, C-122/99 P and 125/99 P D v Council [2001] ECR I-4319; AG Jacobs, 22 March 2001, Case C-270/99P Z v EP; AG Stix-Hackl, 31 May 2001, Case C-49/00 Commission v. Italy; AG Jacobs, 14 June 2001, Case C-377/98 Netherlands v. Council; AG Geelhoed 5 July 2001, Case C-413/99 Baumbast; AG Leger, 1 July 2001, Case C-309/99 Wouters; AG Leger 10 July 2001, Case C-353/99P Hautala; AG Geelhoed, 12 July 200, Case C-313/99 Mulligan; AG Stix-Hackl, 12 July 2001, Case C-160/00 Nilsson; AG Stix-Hackl, 13 September

2001, Case C-60/00 Carpenter; AG Stix-Hackl, 13 September 2001, Case C-459/99 MRAX; AG Mischo 20 September 2001, Cases C-20/00 and 64/00 Booker Aquaculture; AG Stix-Hackl, 27 November 2001, Case C-210/00 Kaserei; AG J-Colomer 3 December 2001, C-208/00 Uberseering.

32. See for example, Case T-54/99 *Max Mobil Telekommunikation Service GmbH*, paragraph 48, 30 January 2002.

33. European Convention on Human Rights Act 2003 (signed 30 June 2003).

34. Ulrich Haltern, 'Europe Goes Camper – the EU Charter of Fundamental Rights from a Consumerist Perspective' CONWEB 3/2001.

35. Eugene Regan, *The Charter of Fundamental Rights* (Institute of European Affairs 2002), p. 12.

36. The Irish Centre for European Law held a conference in September 2000, leading to the publication *Fundamental Social Rights – Current European Legal Protection and the Challenge of the EU Charter of Fundamental Rights* (ICEL No 28 2001).

37. *Sinnott v. Minister for Education* [2001] 2, IR 545.

38. Gerard Hogan, *Irish Times*, 20 February 2003.

39. Eugene Regan, *Irish Times*, 28 February 2003.

40. 'Thoughts on the EU Charter of Fundamental Rights' Institute of European Affairs, 4 March 2003, and paper presented at the ICEL Fourth Annual Congress, 'The Making of a Constitution for Europe', 24 May 2003.

8. IRELAND AND EUROPE: EMBRACING CHANGE
BERTIE AHERN

1. An Taoiseach, Seán Lemass, TD, Opening Statement to EEC Council of Ministerat Talks on Ireland's Application, Brussels, 18 January, 1962. Quoted in Dermot Keogh, *Ireland and Europe 1919–1989: A Diplomatic and Political History* (Hibernian University Press), p. 233.

Acknowledgments

AnnMarie O'Callaghan of RTÉ commissioned the Thomas Davis Lecture series of the same name as this book – *Ireland and the European Union* – and brought an ongoing level of care and commitment to its development and completion.

Séamus Hosey, again of RTÉ, who produced the radio series within deadlines that would have frightened many, energized the productions by his professional and literary vigilance and expertise.

The Commission of the European Union generously supported the production of the radio series. Peter Doyle, the Director of the Commission's Dublin offices, and Harry O'Connor, the Director of Information, were strong advocates of the application for this support and were constantly helpful in the development of the series.

Lilliput Press, in particular Antony Farrell and Marsha Swan, were once again such a pleasant and professional publishing house to work with. Their constant good humour and unflappability made this project seem easier than I know it was.

Commissioner David Byrne brings both an Irish and a European dimension to his foreword. His reflections on the timeliness of this publication in the context of the imminent enlargement of the EU are much appreciated.

My seven fellow contributors brought variety and verve to

their broadcast and published scripts. They once again prove the old adage, 'If you want a job done, ask a busy person.' I am very grateful to them all for their participation in the project.

The Communicating Europe Initiative of the Department of Foreign Affairs and the Research Committee of St Patrick's College, Drumcondra, provided funding to assist this publication and my indebtedness to them and Urban Institute Ireland is acknowledged.

I have taught a course on Europe over the last thirty years to some thousands of geography students and I am glad of an opportunity to publicly thank them for their ideas and reflections on their Europe – a Europe that is constantly changing and reinventing itself.

Europe, ultimately, is about people. Four very special people have offered encouragement when they thought it necessary and have been quietly supportive when they deemed it prudent. To Norma, my wife, and our children, David, Marianne and James, I again say thank you.

Notes on Contributors

Bertie Ahern, TD, An Taoiseach

David Begg, General Secretary of the Irish Congress of Trade Unions

Cathryn Costello, Fellow and Tutor in EC and Public Law, Worcester College, Oxford University

Professor Michael Cronin, Director of the Centre for Translation and Textual Studies, Dublin City University

Dr Garret FitzGerald, author and former Taoiseach

Jim Hourihane, Department of Geography, St Patrick's College, Drumcondra, Dublin

Dr Brigid Laffan, Jean Monnet Professor of European Politics, University College Dublin

Dr Larry Siedentop, Department of Politics, Keble College, Oxford University